DEVELOPMENT AS ATTITUDE

How National Progress is shaped by Leadership Philosophy and Citizens' Orientation

Adonis & Abbey Publishers Ltd
24 Old Queen Street, London SW1H 9HP United Kingdom
Website: http://www.adonis-abbey.com
E-mail Address: editor@adonis-abbey.com

Nigeria:
Plot 2560, Hassan Musa Katsina Street, Asokoro, Abuja, Nigeria
Tel: +234 (0) 7058078841/08052035034
Website: http://www.adonis-abbey.com
E-mail Address: editor@adonis-abbey.com

British Library Cataloguing-in-Publication Data
A catalogue record for this book is available from the British Library

ISBN: 9781913976262

DEVELOPMENT AS ATTITUDE

How National Progress is shaped by Leadership Philosophy and Citizens' Orientation

Osita Ogbu

Table of Contents

Part IV: Development and Insecurity

Chapter Ten
Chapter Eleven

Part V: Development Strategies In The Face Of Global Disruption

Chapter Twelve
Chapter Thirteen

Foreword

This book joins many others in awakening our consciousness to the unfinished task of charting a sustained course towards Nigeria's, indeed, Africa's development. It uniquely identifies attitude- knowledge, values and philosophy- of leaders as key to national progress. Leadership has so many dimensions. But a leader's attitude governs her knowledge architecture and use, both in its authenticity and contextual relevance, and the values she promotes. Development involves an evaluation of alternative values, courses of action, conflicting interests and taking decisions that best serve the interest of the nation. This analysis of options, resolution of our contradictions, sense of justice and equity, honesty and pragmatism and decisions therefrom are significantly influenced by the deep-held philosophy of the leader. More importantly, the ability to mobilize the citizens for the urgent task of development, often involving sacrifices, will depend on how contagious the optimistic, enthusiastic and impactful attitude of the leader is. This scarcely charted path is the value this book brings to our development discourse.

And this book is not a leadership book but a book on development practice. I am amazed at how the author was able to successfully weave the core theme of this book, leadership philosophy and citizens' orientation, across many significant development challenges in Nigeria. From issues of Justice and equity, national integration and citizenship, leadership recruitment, national planning, inclusive growth, inequality, global disruptions, management of the national economy to insecurity, the author directs the minds of the readers to the inevitable conclusion that addressing these challenges successfully, hence national progress, depends on the attitude of the leaders and consciousness of the citizens that follow in tow.

I must say that I am not surprised. Prof. Osita Ogbu is an economist but he is also a development theoretician and practitioner. He is a true social scientist, with excellent analytical skills, who is able to reflect and write across disciplinary boundaries. It is a testament to his rigorous training, his exposure and working experiences across the globe in significant international institutions where challenges of development are examined from a multi-disciplinary perspective. His experience at the highest policymaking level in Nigeria provided him the opportunity to understand the nuances of Nigeria's leadership and development challenges and how to untangle our contradictions. The book is at once a development text and a policymaker's guide.

This book is coming out at a time when the citizens of Nigeria and elsewhere in Africa are agitating for a new set of leaders with progressive values and philosophy. It will inform and shape the debate in an intelligent manner and would greatly enrich the readers.

I thank Prof. Ogbu for being a great associate and friend, and for asking me to write this foreword to a great book.

Dr. Goodluck Ebele Jonathan, GCFR
President of the Federal Republic of Nigeria (2010-2015)
Chairman, GEJ Foundation

Preface

African development has been elusive; a resource-rich continent in constant search of how to address its many developmental challenges and lifts its people out of poverty. Many policies have been suggested and implemented. Several models of development have been analysed and copied, even if not entirely. Many external institutions of knowledge have descended on the continent with new ideas on how to deal with the constraining factors and have cajoled their implementation. Development partners have come in and carved up the territories in accordance with their respective interests. More or less aid has been suggested. Institutions and markets have been created. New forms of governance have been implemented. Democracy and openness advocated and implemented. Leaders have been changed. Our cultures mutilated and blamed. Prayers have also been offered. All of this was futile. But we shall not give up.

This book joins many others in seeking contemporary solutions to Africa's development dilemma. From my many years as a student, teacher, scholar, researcher, and policymaker, I have reached the inescapable conclusion that ATTITUDE, defined as knowledge and ideology (values and philosophy), is what shapes a nation's development trajectory. It is not any kind of knowledge. You must have reasons for knowing, and that knowledge must have an ideologically relevant content because knowledge is not value-free. The knowledge must be authentic in its consonance with a nation's historical and contextual reality. When some donors insist that aid must be coupled with their own ideas, they violate this very principle. Those who are in need of the aid would take the aid and implement half-heartedly the imported ideas that have been forced on them. And then there is the other side of the coin. The recipient's philosophy that donors know best and by accepting, albeit reluctantly, the money that came with the ideas, conveys the wrong attitude and everything that is wrong with Africa's development philosophy: it is reckless, lacks deep thinking and interrogative capacity, and reinforces self-doubt. Any nation travelling the route of self-doubt can never develop. You have to own what you know and develop what you know, even if you deliberately use other people's ideas to augment yours. Choices are, therefore, driven by attitude. And making the right choices is what development is all about. Leaders make these choices on behalf of the citizens. And if these leaders are not guided by the right ideology, nations stagnate. Leaders need legitimacy, discipline, and must have a certain fearless, contagious optimism and self-belief to mobilize citizens, overcome challenges, resolve internal contradictions and engineer transformation.

This book is not a conventional development studies text. It did not take the conventional topics and group them into chapters or try to analyse them. This is a collection of my researched lectures delivered to various audiences. These lectures are accessible, practical, and at the same time thought-provoking. It is useful as a development studies text, for general reading by social scientists, including economists, and everyone interested in understanding Africa's development challenges. The topics are diverse, but the common thread running through them is an examination of leadership and citizens' attitudes in the context of the subject matter in terms of the advancement or lack thereof of Nigeria's (Africa's) development. Its unique feature is the variety of multi-national examples that reinforce the theme, making it an important book in comparative development experience. Countries that have developed or are developing have or have had leaders with the right attitudinal disposition to their society's progress and have instilled discipline among the citizens.

Given that the lectures are delivered at different times to different audiences, there are some repetitions in the use of certain statements and examples to elucidate key subject matters. In particular, the lessons that can be drawn from the transformation of Singapore and Malaysia and the exemplary attitude of the leaders were used to address the leadership issues in some of the chapters. As a social scientist concerned with the significant ills of inequality, one can also understand the emphasis I placed on this subject matter as I reflect on the problematique of constructing inclusive development and the creation of shared prosperity in some of the chapters. The advantage, in spite of the repetitions, is that each chapter is autonomous and can be read on its own. Even when certain data may be dated, the important lessons should not be lost on the reader.

From economic policy making—national planning, budgetary choices, inclusive growth, preparing for the fourth industrial revolution, structural transformation—to building resilience, creating national cohesion and citizenship, and dealing with insecurity, the book underscores the absence of a guiding attitudinal philosophy among African leaders that percolates among the followers. The absence of such an underpinning positive attitude, serving as a guard rail, means that there is either no motion or that it is directionless. Even if this is described as the absence of elite consensus, such consensus can only be built on the bedrock of common ideology. In a fast-paced world with accelerating technology, this ideology or attitude is required as an anchor to withstand the blistering associated with globalisation and its sometimes unforeseen and undesirable outcomes. Without a strong positive attitude, how else can the leaders understand the importance of domestic production and consumption of knowledge, the relevance of technology and innovation, the role of planning, the advancement of local content, the importance of shared vision, the proper management of institutions, the dangers of inequality, capacity building that addresses the nation's needs, the infrastructural choices, the assessment of risks, and the insistence on developing on one's own terms. Even the ability to receive, process, and adapt new information for the good of society is shaped by ideology. These and many more, critical for Africa's development, are shaped by the attitude of leaders as managers of conflicting values and interests and the philosophy they instill among the citizens. This book is concerned with these issues.

I am grateful to my teachers at both the University of Nigeria and Howard University who reinforced my ability to "reason in three dimensions" according to one of them, who taught me about knowledge and ideology and from whom I gained the confidence and audacity to think differently and purposefully with respect to Africa's development. Some of the statements at the beginning of the chapters without attribution are mine, as an expression of my confidence in what I know—the audacity of knowledge. The opportunity of serving the government of Nigeria at the highest level and my many engagements with the private sector exposed me to the attitudes of our leaders at various cadres and informed some of the views expressed in this book. These invaluable lessons humbled the economist in me and forced me to acknowledge and seek answers to our development challenges in other disciplines. This is therefore a book written by a social scientist, a development practitioner, rather than an economist. The book raises the age-old question of the usefulness of organizing knowledge along strict disciplinary silos.

PART ONE
Attitude and Transformation

CHAPTER ONE

Development as Attitude

First, development is an outcome of a transformative attitude embedded in a shared vision espoused and driven by an intelligent leader as he or she envisions a new progressive society where shared prosperity, justice, equity, fairness, merit, and equality of opportunity are the cornerstones.

Second, development arises from a creative attitude among citizens that prioritises knowledge, discipline, honesty, trust, hard work, productivity, demand for accountability from leaders, and a cooperative attitude that does not diminish individual or group excellence.

Third, development is a result of attitudinal re-orientation that structures a productive partnership between the states on the one hand and the citizens as well as private sector on the other through the creation of institutions that harness, in a transformative way, state, citizen, and private sector resources towards the delivery of public services as well as public and private goods in a manner that ennobles citizens.

Ideology is what ties the three things productively together. In a fast-paced world, ideology, defined as a set of values and knowledge, has become even more imperative for a leader and a nation. You don't just have to know; you also have to have reasons for knowing, a core set of values serving as a prism for reflection and proper interpretation of what you know, and the inspiration to share and advocate your knowledge. It is this knowledge and values (ideology) that shape ATTITUDE towards development. Development would occur or not occur depending on whether the actors (leaders and citizens), in their thoughts, actions, and preoccupations have proper attitudinal orientation. Attitude becomes the basis for priority-setting, ambition, decisions, policies, and followership. If a leader has no defined attitude about how to transform his society, he will push in any direction or no direction at all. And society is worse for it.

In a democracy, the contemporary utility or ordinary relevance of the concept of ideology lies in the understanding of the true sovereignty of the people as the custodian and beneficiary of power — in understanding that the shepherd is not the owner of the flock. Or as the Igbos in Nigeria would rhetorically ask of their leaders, "fa ama onye fa na achulu efi?" Do they know who the master is? The citizens or the godfathers? The money bags? Questions that continually underscore that the practise of democracy in this clime is significantly impaired.

I went to a very good school for my post-graduate studies — Howard University in Washington, DC—both my Masters and Ph.D. in economics were obtained there between 1983 and 1988. It may not be the best school for econometrics or mathematical economics, but it taught me a very important lesson. Economic knowledge, like any other disciplinary knowledge, must be about people. I learned that people's or society's stories must inform models or the numbers, and that we must interpret the numbers heartfully, purposefully, and with empathy and humility. After all, economics is all about what we don't know about the economy, made worse by technology and globalisation. According to Thomas Friedman, "it takes caring to ignite caring; and it takes empathy to ignite empathy". And the world needs a caring and empathic society. It was at Howard University that a distinguished professor of economics, Koffi Kissi Dompere, taught me that knowledge without a proper ideological orientation is not only useless but can also be dangerous. He taught me about the social production of knowledge and the self-motivation and unconscious distortion that surround the use of knowledge, especially "in perpetuating power relations". "You must define for what purpose your knowledge exists", he would often admonish. Is your knowledge and understanding liberating or enslaving for the plurality of the people? So, you may have a Ph.D. or be a professor, and you may have knowledge but lack understanding because your attitude, ideology, and values require significant change, reorientation, or attitude adjustment.

It is often true with those in power in Africa. Many lack knowledge but refuse to acknowledge it, disobeying the basic principles of leadership—knowing what you don't know. President Obama wrote, in this respect, "don't be afraid to ask question when you need it. I do that every day. Asking for help isn't a sign of weakness; it's a sign of strength. It shows you have the courage to admit when you don't know something and to learn something new". Others have knowledge but lack understanding, and almost all of them have attitude and ideological issues because they have failed to recognise who their masters are, the citizens! How does a public servant become a public master? Does a governor know that he has been recruited by the citizens of his state to serve them? Is the State Assembly aware that the citizens have entrusted them with the responsibility of keeping an eye on their commonwealth and holding the shepherd accountable? The shepherd and those whose constitutional responsibility it is to monitor and check the activities of the shepherd need a new, attitude, understanding, and reorientation. Otherwise, we will not make any progress. I once heard a governor say at a political rally that we should thank a local government chairman because he built a road —after all, if he hadn't, what would we, the citizens of that local government, have done if instead he misappropriated the funds? It was a very insulting, unfortunate, and ignorant comment from an unaccountable leader. Did he build the road with his father's money or the citizens' money? No wonder we send delegations to thank a governor for constructing a road as if it were built with personal resources. But the citizens themselves must resist the enslavement and assert themselves as the owners of the commonwealth. Unfortunately, the elite and the so-called intellectuals now lack the interrogating power and proper ideological orientation that they once had, and they are now doing "song and dance" for those in power as ordinary citizens watch helplessly. The elite and the intellectuals need attitude adjustments. The same elite and the so-called intellectuals have misled the citizens to believe that, "onye bu igu ka ewu na eso", a goat follows anyone that is carrying a palm frond. No questions asked? Even when the palm frond may be your last supper, and I ask, are we now goats? Have we lost any discerning sense? Does the source of the palm frond matter? What of the integrity, character, and competence of the bearer of the palm frond?

Drinking from the school of thought as espoused by my Howard University professor, coupled with significant and wide-ranging interactions with scholars across Africa, I came up with the concept of the African Intellectual Freedom Fighters. The idea that we need a core of Africans with knowledge, understanding, values, and ideology - the right attitude- who are willing to take the risk and bear the cost of using that knowledge and understanding to liberate our people, the Africans. If development, according to Amartya Sen, is "freedom from hunger, disease, ignorance, homelessness, tyranny"; if development involves subduing nature; advancing the welfare of citizens, creating productive economic opportunities; or if development, as I stated somewhere else, is the resolution of our many contradictions such as schooling without learning; consuming what we don't produce; many jobbers without jobs; growth without development and democracy without the people's participation and freedom and restoration of the dignity of man, it would require intellectuals in a very broad sense, those I call intellectual freedom fighters to generate knowledge, deploy programmes and activities, authentic African solutions to the challenges. But it is not just any knowledge or idea. And it is not intellectual. Freedom fighters are confident, courageous, fearless, selfless, honorable, ideological, purpose-driven, futuristic, and have the power of conviction. I was therefore looking for a corps of intellectuals with these authentic attributes. Those who are certain of their knowledge; those who believe that what they know matters, and are not afraid that their conclusions will offend certain masters; those who are not afraid of jeopardising future contracts or career; convinced that knowledge generating centres exist in any part of the world and willing to challenge so called settled, stylised, sometimes, ahistorical facts doled out as gospels by certain western and global institutions; can make a distinction between material poverty and intellectual ability; convinced that Africa's development cannot be engineered by some external force; aware that useful partnerships are built on the strength of domestic knowledge and horned expertise, devoid of self-doubt; that self-appraisal is not the same as persistent negative criticism; aware that knowledge is not ideological or value neutral.

The current debates and discussions around Nigeria's practise of democracy call for an urgent need for these intellectual freedom fighters to get involved. Around the corridor, all we hear is how governors are jostling to select their successors. It is very interesting. Very unfortunate! The main kernel of the argument is that previous ones did it, so why not the current ones? And I ask, is this how we are going to advance democracy, human dignity, and progress? That the choice of who becomes a councilor; a local government chairman, a House of Representative member, a senator or the governor is now in the hands of one person, the governor? This partly explains why all the so-called elected officials do not respect the sovereignty of the citizens, who believe that power belongs to them, because of the distorted view that power is exercised by one man. And we are not a monarchy. So, we must perpetuate and celebrate that which is wrong because it has always been so? Ndigbo na asi "na ejioro ajo ife amatu", there is no moral virtue in repeating an unfortunate act despite the outcome. You can always reverse your journey if you are going in the wrong direction.

We are going deeper in the wrong direction. Our democracy is in peril. Those with money purchase political power and, through corrupt means, acquire more money and further perpetuate themselves in power. If the office holder is not rich, he must then be sponsored by a "godfather", to whom he would be making returns. In either scenario, the citizens are not the sovereign, and addressing their needs is secondary. After all, re-election is not dependent on performance. But something else is more worrisome. When primary elections throw up candidates who do not reflect the will of the people but the will of one person, often the governor of the state, of what value is an election where the candidates do not represent any real choice? It is then the case of the "devil and the deep blue sea". While millions of public dollars are spent on conducting elections every four years and the international community cheers, I see this selection phenomenon as the weakest link in the democratic practise in Nigeria. And it may be its death knell if major corrective actions are not taken. When we persistently insist on economic reforms without a concomitant emphasis on political reforms, we fail to acknowledge that politics is superior to economics. If there is no virtue in the politics of today, how can there be virtue in the politics of tomorrow? Because like begets like. It is, therefore, not difficult to understand why there is a high degree of apathy among the electorates, engendering the feeling of "its same old same old". It is also for this this reason, as well as the enormous entry barrier erected by money politics, that good people with the right attitude have stayed out of politics, to the detriment of society.

Tied to the proper ideological orientation are the issues of values and morality. Make it any way you can, but make it the currency in town. Those who demand that our politics, governance, and policies be value and morality-laden are labelled as losers. But exerting influence on the basis of moral authority is better than exercising authority on the basis of the office you occupy. Those who elect to serve must think beyond the office they occupy and bring lasting values into governance. They must lead on the basis of morality and integrity, on the basis of what is good or bad for the majority of the citizens. The progress of society, *Oganiru*, is premised on these fundamental truth and principles. This is precisely why we need attitude adjustment, reorientation, and refocusing on people in our policies, actions, and strategies.

Attitude, Institutions, and Progress

Why do I keep speaking about the majority? To make progress, we must uplift the majority out of poverty and significantly reduce inequality. And why should we be worried about rising inequality? In the book, *The Spirit Level: Why Greater Equality Makes Societies Stronger*,[1] Richard Wilkinson and Kate Pickett underscore the importance of inclusiveness and reduced inequality in any transformation agenda. They note that "the transformation of our society is a project in which we all have a shared interest. Greater equality is the gateway to a society capable of improving the quality of life for all of us and an essential step in the development of a sustainable economic system." In essence, the great inequality we are experiencing in Nigeria must be seen as a hindrance to the transformation agenda; and policies must be targeted at creating greater equality or else the transformation would be at best fragile and, most likely, unsustainable. Needless to say, the violence all around us, partly a manifestation of this great inequality, can hardly allow any transformation to take root.

To deal with this inequality requires a significant attitude adjustment and an empathetic leadership philosophy —an appreciation that the wealth of the nation is for all; that equal opportunity means that we must return to rebuilding public primary and secondary schools and public health facilities. The children of the driver attended the same school as the children of the master when we were growing up. There were no private schools of significance. We had good public and mission schools. Now, the wealthy and those who can afford it have fled public schools, leaving the majority of them in deplorable conditions with children schooling without learning. When the poor are not given the opportunity, through education, to improve their capacity and capability, inequality will widen, with all the attendant consequences.

Robert Reich, a professor of public policy at the University of California, Berkley reminds us of some of the consequences. He stated: "Inequality undermines the trust, solidarity, and mutuality on which the responsibilities of citizenship depend."[2] So how can you have responsible citizens where the majority feels excluded? When one law applies to the poor and another to the wealthy? How can you have mutuality and solidarity when every rich Nigerian man dies in London or Paris and every poor man dies in his forsaken village or urban slum? We need a serious attitude adjustment.

Attitude Adjustment, Reorientation, and Shame: The Japanese Experience

In 1945, some 77 years ago, Japan, the great empire, surrendered to the United States and allied forces. It was a difficult but inevitable act. By culture and temperament, Japanese people have no surrender in their dictionaries, especially in their military dictionaries. This was a proud nation with a race-based imperialist ideology that exported costly wars across Asia and the Pacific. As reported by Marx Fisher in the Atlantic Magazine (1998), the war "cost nearly 20 million Asian lives, more than 3.1 million Japanese lives, and more than 60,000 Western Allied lives."[3] Japan at that time had a leader, Emperor Hirohito, who was thought to be divine and whose words were obeyed. He was a "paradigm of moral excellence" and a "living embodiment of Japan", which enabled him to command so much respect, authority, and followership. Even though he rarely spoke publicly, the Japanese believe that their emperor would want them to fight till the last person, "a commitment to death", to protect the sanctity of their nation and their dignity.

On this day in August 1945, the unthinkable happened. Emperor Hirohito, the 124th Emperor of Japan, in a 4-minute radio address, ordered the Japanese army, wherever they may be, to surrender unconditionally to the allied forces of America, Great Britain, China, and the Soviet Union, marking the end of the Second World War. This surrender came after President Truman of the United States decided to use the atomic bomb to destroy the cities of Hiroshima and Nagasaki. The Emperor knew that the enemy had raised the stake, and Japan was unable to compete. The Japanese surrender was not simply a surrender to the American government or to the allied forces. It was not simply a surrender to the courage of President Harry Truman; it was a- surrender to the superior technology and innovation of the United States, the atomic bomb. In his address, the Emperor stated that "the enemy has begun to employ a new and most cruel bomb"; a bomb that President Truman described as "a new weapon of unusual destructive force."

In surrendering in shame and humility to this superior weapon brought about by advances in science, technology, and innovation, the Emperor exhorted his people to rise to the new challenge of overcoming all obstacles with superior technology and knowledge. More than the surrender, his words and the attitude they engendered marked the turning point in Japanese transformation and technological advancement. "We have resolved to pave the way for a grand peace for all generations to come by enduring the unendurable and suffering what is insufferable… we are always with you, our good and loyal subjects, relying on your sincerity and integrity."[4] He went further to urge hard work and creativity to overcome this shame. "Unite your total strength to be devoted to the construction of the future. Cultivate the ways of rectitude, nobility of spirit, and work with resolution so that you may enhance the innate glory of the Imperial State and keep pace with the progress of the world."[5] He said all of these in four minutes. But it changed the mission and the identity of the Japanese.

It was this surrender and the shame it brought to the Emperor and Japan that changed the attitude of the Japanese people and government and produced one of the greatest economic transformations in human history. At the end of the war, Japan was near collapse, with half of their cities destroyed and more than 30 percent of the residents rendered homeless while disease and starvation were rampant. In rebuilding, Japan created new institutions, new sets of incentives, and promulgated a new constitution that removed the powers of the Emperor. In 1946, the Emperor declared that he was not divine after all and moved closer to his people.

Let us spend a few moments on the concept of shame; that sense of inadequacy "in relation to a valued goal or ideal"; what the psychologist Stephen Krugman refers to as "a painful self-awareness… that arises when there is a negative discrepancy between ideal and (self) experience". In other words, when a nation's ideals or goals are within reach, and less endowed, comparator, or competitor nations achieve those goals, a sense of shame should ensue. Properly deconstructed, shame can trigger a positive response. Within this construct, shame provides the impetus for reconstructing the incentives, institutions, and attitudes required to attain and surpass the goals and ideals of that nation. It becomes the rallying cry for the leadership and citizens to make the appropriate sacrifices for transformation. That is what Japan did.

Japan not only kept pace with the progress of the world; it became, in many respects, the world's leader technologically. They had the will to confront their inglorious past, wrote a new democratic constitution, created inclusive economic and political institutions with new sets of incentives, and reduced the powers of the Emperor. Similar arguments are currently going on in Nigeria with respect to constitutional amendments. Japan is a modern, techno-industrial power, a democratic country at peace with herself and her neighbors. While many factors contributed to Japan's economic miracle, the sense of shame, to "suffer the insufferable," especially in the hands of Americans due to their superior knowledge, the attitude it engendered, and the deep reflection and challenge that came from the Emperor's words, were a major turning point in Japan's rebirth.

Need for Attitude Adjustment and Reorientation Among Leaders and Followers: Other Examples

This may be dated, but it illustrates an important point. We can say that Britain witnessed a rebirth in 2012. The kind of rebirth that allowed it to put on a world-class Olympics in London, both in terms of organisation and medal haul. Events in both business and politics were beginning to mar the image of this great country. From the crisis in the banking industry arising from the "malpractice of cheating their customers" and the manipulation of rates and insurance covers on credit to the breach of public trust by politicians who were cheating on their claims, Eddie Iroh, writing on Britain: The Re-Birth of a Nation, in the Thisday of August 15, 2012 captured the transformation that is taking place in Britain and the attitude and incentives required for such transformation. He contrasted it with what we currently have in Nigeria. The new attitude and incentives in Britain came from the embarrassment and shame caused by conduct of their political and business leaders and the need to punish offenders and reward good deeds. According to Iroh, "… you see a nation (Britain) that is truly embarrassed by the misconduct of its trustees in politics and business, the disgrace of its traditional values, and its genuine effort to bring the miscreants to justice or to take justice to them. You see a nation that is genuinely remorseful; not one (Nigeria) that will swear to "leave no stone un-turned" and then leaves every stone un-turned… vows to "fish out" the culprits and then hides the culprits…promises no sacred cows and finds a safe haven for the sacred cows." As long as we are not remorseful or ashamed of the actions of our public figures and do not take steps to bring them to justice, as long as our democratic and justice institutions are weak, we would be on the transformation path without transforming.

When we suffer shame, do we retreat and reconstruct our institutions to respond and conquer? It would appear that we no longer suffer shame… every performance no matter how abysmal, does not arouse a sense of anger —the kind of anger that allows a nation to say, "never again", the kind of anger that allows you to create institutions, new incentives, and the new values required to attain greater heights — the kind of the anger that allows a nation to meet the expectations of her citizens. That we have Boko Haram, kidnapping and all other forms of militancy, and indeed, corruption and a high level of poverty, should trigger anger and shame, and consequently, a national response to these negative characterisations that mar the image of the country and stunt our development. When a nation has no shame, it would assume that transformation would occur simply by decreeing it and by happenstance or by the chronological age of the nation, lacking the incentives, the resolution, the nobility of spirit, the attitude, the "sense of purpose", and the patriotism to rise to the challenge and seize the opportunity to "keep pace with the progress of the world" and to conquer.

It is not just a leadership issue; it is also a followership issue. In an interview in the Thisday published on Monday, September 3, 2012, the Trade Union Congress President General, Mr. Peter Esele, lamented the loss of good values and accountability in our system and how programmes designed to help people are sabotaged by ordinary people. The TUC has a set of buses on the streets of Lagos, bought with borrowed money. In one instance, an operator who brought in revenue of 8 million naira also tendered an expense bill of 11 million naira. What kind of business would survive under this kind of mathematics? What kind of mindset allows this? A mind set of "it is my turn to chop and I have nothing else at stake"? TUC have found out the holes and have begun to plug them. In one instance, those in charge bought fake diesel, and TUC had to flush the entire system. Sometimes the fuel is stolen. In Peter Esele's words, "These are the things that are happening among followers, later we accuse our leaders of corruption… we have to change our values or else this country would not change." Indeed, we have to change our values and attitude, or else this country will not transform. There have been similar lamentations about our legislators, civil servants, ministers, and clergy men— leaders and followers alike.

Writing a commentary on the science of success in The Thisday Newspaper of August 29, 2012, Chris Ngwodo, spurred by our recent poor outing at the 2012 London Olympics, captures what I would rather characterise as the science of transformation. He states emphatically that "for successful countries, success is a science—an outcome empirically determined by rational systems and structures based on the consistent application of efforts and resources and the cultivation of habits of excellence… for unsuccessful countries, success is a miracle, an act of God…and excellence is a magical occurrence originating not from human exertion but from the realm of the unknown." He continued, "Miracles are permissible metaphors in personal narratives, but they are unknown in nation-building and development." With all due respect, nations do not pray themselves into development and transformation, as many Nigerians and leaders believe. We take it literally, that "with God all things are possible", yes possible for those who are prepared. You cannot dwell in sin and hope to go to heaven; you cannot destroy your institutions, cultivate habits and values that promote decadence and hope to transform; you cannot have citizens who have no sense of loyalty to their nation and workers who are not professionally managed to give their best and expect the miracle of development.

The Role of Human Resource Managers in a Transformation Agenda

From the Singaporean experiences, as we will see later, and the Japanese experiences, we can clearly discern the critical human elements that represent the platform for transformation. To transform is to re-engineer culturally: to create new values, a new incentive structure, new habits, and new systems. It is to plan for the glorious future, in which everyone has a stake. It means increased productivity; it means out-competing other nations; it means getting the best from our workers; it means cultivating the habit of excellence among our worker force. It also means creating a new work ethic and a new working relationship between workers and managers, resulting in an industrial harmony that creates a win-win situation for all stakeholders. It means innovation in the workplace, the deployment of new technology and new processes, and the continuous search for "other sources of competitive advantage", including flexibility in human resource deployment and management of the relatively high speed of adjustment. It means building an inclusive workplace in a multicultural or multiethnic environment. Ultimately, all of these would translate to a higher standard of living for all, not just some.

The new human resource expert is, therefore, a patriot, putting the interests of his or her organisation and the nation before his. The HR expert must have the skills for creating an inclusive environment that builds a team without diluting individual creativity, that creates a sense of belonging for all, and at the same time searches for and nurtures talent. Singapore was adamant about creating a peaceful multi-ethnic society that encourages and rewards excellence. It is the role of HR experts to to foster employee loyalty to the organization, to work tirelessly to align the goals of the individual worker with those of the organization, and to promote fairness, equity, and worker appreciation among management and political leaders. In Nigeria, these issues are at the heart of our low productivity and require a human resource management strategy driven by experts with new skills who are recognised and acknowledged by management and leaders as important drivers of the transformation process.

There are key elements of this strategy that are worthy of note. First, recruitment policies must emphasise merit [skills and knowledge] and job security, which promotes employee commitment, flexibility, and loyalty while not guaranteeing lifetime employment. Second, the strategy must emphasise training as a necessary investment in building a productive workforce with a competitive advantage within the context of workers as "life-long learners." Third is the issue of an equitable compensation structure that addresses the issues of attraction, retention, commitment, cooperativeness, loyalty, involvement, and patriotism of the workforce. Fourth, the issue of harmony in industrial relations is critical for sustainable transformation, requiring the skills to mediate between restive unions and management in times when workers would be asked to make sacrifices. How do we carry workers along in the decision-making process and get them involved in solving problems? It is these HR strategies that produce highly competitive organisations—the kinds of organisations, public and private, that drive the change required for transformation.

The HR manager is the arbiter of trust in any organisation, the custodian of confidential information, the counselor and confidant of employees, and someone who builds on his or her own character to negotiate trust among the workers and between workers and management, a critical requirement for strong commitment to organisations and a low conflict relationship between top managers and leadership, the representative of the workers (unions), and the workers. But what if the HR manager lacks the character to perform this important function, to be a role model, to be trustworthy? What if the environment imposes a different set of incentives on the human resource expert?

Our recruitment process is fraught with corruption. From the advertisement that is not worth the paper it is printed on to the mock interview process that fulfils the requirements of the process after the candidates have been selected by the bosses. Sometimes we know that the experts are used to facilitate this process when they put their interests above those of the system they are supposed to serve, obviously against the principles of the Chattered Institute of Personnel Management. In retention, discipline, and promotion of staff, we witness corruption and nepotism as we wonder aloud where the professional human resource managers are. This is a rhetorical question because we know where they are. Many have not been allowed to do their jobs as professionals with bosses that serve as recruitment agencies, disciplinarians, and promotion experts. The Nigerian boss is a chief, an all-knowing chief. But true professionals do rise up to their chiefs, making their professional views known, taking measured risks, and not allowing the system to overwhelm them to the point of surrender. A true professional would make the appropriate sacrifices required for transformation.

We must therefore realise that as we focus on corruption as embezzlement of funds, mismanagement of funds, or more generally, illicit financial flows, we must be equally concerned about corruption of the systems. In particular, we must be concerned about systems that affect the productivity of workers, their values and attitudes, and their loyalty both to the organisation and to the nation. By addressing these values and attitudes, new leadership would emerge. The kind of leadership that creates change, in both the public and private domains, would create a new ethos, a new work ethic, new sets of incentives, and new institutions that would put Nigeria on a sustainable transformation path.

We are a different people, but we shall play by the universal rules that transformed Singapore, created a new Japan, and are reshaping Britain. There is hope on the horizon if we all join hands, with the will to confront what is wrong with our past and the will to shape a glorious future for all, realising that our unity as a nation may be tested but cannot be broken. In the words of Mahatma Gandhi, "Strength does not come from physical capacity. It comes from an indomitable will. We must become the change we want to see. To believe in something and not live it, is dishonest." May God help us to be honest.

Development and the Ideology of Partnership and Cooperation

I have reflected over President Barack Obama's statement in his inaugural address on the 20th of January, 2008: 'For they have forgotten what this country has already done; what free men and women can achieve when imagination is joined to common purpose, and necessity to courage."[6] - Many times and felt that its simplicity should not becloud the power of the message. In organising my thoughts about this section of this chapter, I felt very strongly that this was an important statement requiring serious commentary as it relates to the current socio-economic and political affairs of any nation in search of its renaissance. I have, for convenience, called this ideology of creative partnership. The message is that the any sub-national competitive spirit must be met with our traditional value of cooperation; otherwise, the imperatives of modern business and the new style of political competition would diminish our individual achievements and stunt the economic and political development of the sub-national.

I felt that Obama was talking to us, Nigerians, and South Eastern Nigerians in particular. Arguably, the South Easterners have never in their history been more individually successful, yet signs of collective failure are all around. They are the technology entrepreneurs or merchants of this nation, yet they have not seen any need to establish a first-rate technology institution east of the Niger to support or upgrade this trade. When individual entrepreneurs have taken the journey of first discovery with the attendant "first mover disadvantages", neither the Southeast States, the governors, communities, or social groups provide any form of support or encouragement.

They have a region without a regional agenda. Who is going to nudge the traders and manufacturers into new and more productive ways? Who is going to teach that cooperation is as important as competition in today's business world? Who would be the arbiter of strong values that had helped the Southeast communities in the past but seem lost on the new generation? The values of hard work, honesty, thrift, trustworthiness, willingness to delay gratification, respect for elders, and respect for education were the hallmarks of the sub-nation. The great thinker, Max Weber's protestant ethics, was a study of the glorious South Eastern days of the past.

In their book, *Culture Matters: How Values Shape Human Progress,*[7] Lawrence Harrison and Samuel Huntington raise an all-important question: "Do we dare to look ourselves in the face, even if it is difficult to recognise ourselves?" This is a question I raise to allow us to interrogate our new ways of being, to evaluate our attitude; appraise our values, and redirect our followership and leadership philosophy. Without a fundamental shift away from the wrong attitude and the poor governance that they entail, our renascent future will elude us, and development and shared prosperity will be a never-ending quest. We must look ourselves in the face.

CHAPTER TWO

Attitude, Leadership Philophy and the Transformation of Society

I went to bed that night convinced they are a different people playing to a different set of rules. - Lee Kuan Yew, 1966

I start this chapter with that sentence from the book, From Third World to First [8], an account by Lee Kuan Yew on how he led the transformation of Singapore, a country Dr. Henry Kissinger described as a "sandbar country with nary a natural resource... destined to become a client state of more powerful neighbors" and rejected by Malaysia because of its insignificance in the 1950s and 1960s, into the great nation it is today. On January 10, 1966, Lee Kuan Yew visited Nigeria in response to the invitation of Nigeria's then Prime Minister, Sir Abubakar Tafawa Balewa, to the Commonwealth Prime Ministers to discuss the unilateral declaration of independence by Rhodesia, a colony ruled by a white minority. After an evening at the banquet organised for the visiting dignitaries and after a long chat with a senior Cabinet Minister in the Balewa government, Lee Kuan Yew concluded that Nigerians "are a different people playing by a different set of rules." We are indeed a different people, but Lee Kuan Yew knew that our values and attitudes were not transformational, and that in our books anything goes, as the cabinet minister was busy making public policy for personal gains and discussing it openly, without equanimity, with a visiting head of government. And we still see the same recklessness and impunity all around us as we turn shameful acts into celebratory events, with attitudes to public office and public property that are least transformational and with citizens whose values and work ethics need serious re-orientation but who are powerless in the face of successive small ruling elites.

Lee Kuan Yew led Singapore from poverty to prosperity in three decades, and his attitude was informed by his "hatred for cruelties on fellow Asians" by the Japanese; his sense of "nationalism and self-respect", his "resentment at being lorded over"; his sense of confidence; an environment that bullied the Chinese minority; and the willingness to rally Singaporeans to the "hardship of going it alone"; and the determination to "build a multi-racial society that would give equality to all citizens". It was an attitude of "hard work, planning, and improvising." In his words, "we cannot afford to forget that public order, personal security, economic and social progress, and prosperity are not the natural order of things and that they depend on the ceaseless effort and attention from an honest and effective government the people must elect." Implying that a government whose attitudes and aspirations must mirror that of the citizens, the informed and patriotic electorate. It means a work force imbued with positive values, willing to give its best, and managed for greater productivity.

If you closely examine both the rhetoric and the reality of Singaporean's transformation, you will understand the underlying policy and attitudinal requirements: hard work, self-determination, pride (or if you like, avoidance of shame), justice and equal opportunity (as embedded in their fair not a welfare society principle), protection of the weak ("giving every citizen a stake in the country and its future"), an uncompromising stance against corruption ("a deep sense of mission to run a clean and effective government"), an attitude of equality before the law and a rule of law with strict enforcement that deterred crime (either organized or random), insistence on high quality education (pursued and nurtured talent and instituted meritocracy), and finally, a sense of self-confidence. When Singapore banned chewing gum in 1992, they were ridiculed in the West as a "nanny" state, but they were confident that they would make people laugh last. In the words of Lee Kuan Yew, "we would have been a grosser, ruder, cruder society had we not made these efforts to persuade our people to change their ways". And change their ways they did to transform their society: from a per capita GDP of USD 400 in 1959 to USD 22, 000 in 1999, and USD 56,532 in 2012. For the same period, Nigeria moved from USD 100 to USD 1,400. Singapore is one of the safest, most peaceful, and cleanest places to live, and poverty is no longer part of the development lexicon of this multi-ethnic nation.

Now compare this renaissance school of thought with our current way of doing business in Nigeria. [In analysing the Singaporean attitude, I picked one of their guiding principles for emphasis because it summarises the fundamental social contract that binds society and, more importantly, that binds the government and the governed. This attitude and principle are summarised in twelve words, "to give every citizen a stake in the country and its future." Do you know what this means? It means that a country has a vision of its future. Not any future, a glorious future. It means that we must put structures, systems, and the right values in place now if this future of abundance is to materialize. It means that if you work as a *mai guard (informal security man), mai ruwa (water seller), okada* rider (motorcycle transporter), wheel barrow pusher, hairdresser, housemaid the government and society care about you. It means that we shall all join hands (led by the government, of course!) to create a society where you are not only able to meet the basic necessities of life, such as food, shelter, and clothing, but that there is a guarantee that your children will be better equipped to be part of and take advantage of the glorious future. It means an attitude towards the public housing that ensures wide-spread ownership for all classes; an attitude towards public school system that guarantees first–class education for the poor; an attitude towards agriculture and other economic activities that build the assets of the poor; it means an attitude of hard work, sacrifice, and vision for a glorious future; a future that will be shared by all, not by a few. When people do not have a stake now or in the future, the required sacrifice for transformation would be resisted. There will be no peace if people do not have a stake; if people do not have a stake, the attitude will be to destroy rather than create; to transform oneself rather than society. The words of George Gilder (1985), the author of The Spirit of Enterprise[9], ring a bell once again: leadership must have an attitude that creates a sense of belonging and shared ownership for followers to make the necessary sacrifices to transform a dry land into an oasis of prosperity.

Let me bring the lesson home. A couple of years ago, I took about 40 senior staff members of a federal ministry to Kaduna for training on character, values and work ethics. Midway through the first day of the training, I asked, somewhat innocuously, "on a scale of 1-10, where does your patriotism lie?" A good many raised their hands and screamed zero. I was dumbfounded and visibly concerned. "Zero", I exclaimed, unsure if I had heard correctly. And the very courageous ones, not minding my sense of angst, still insisted that it was zero. They may not have realised it, but here were senior officers of the federal government, none of whom was below level 12, admitting that they had no loyalty to the nation. Here were officers who are custodians of a portion our national treasure; the ones on whom the government and ordinary citizens rely to articulate and implement government policies that would transform the nation, stating unequivocally that they have no loyalty to that same nation. In short, they have no stake in Nigeria now or in her future. No wonder things are the way they are.

I quickly switched the training to an emotional lecture on patriotism. It occurred to me that patriotism which is "love of and loyalty to one's country"; "an emotional journey of loyalty, allegiance, impartial love, and total obedience to one's country or one's chosen country"; "An awareness of our moral duties to the political community" (Acton, 1972, 163); "pride in one's country's merits and achievements and shame for her lapses and crimes"; "A central moral virtue" (Alasdair MacIntyre) may be confused with loyalty or lack thereof to a government. While someone may dislike a government, one is duty-bound as a citizen to love his or her country. Governments will come and go, but the nation, Nigeria, will remain. But the truth is that many people do not feel good about our country because they have not felt good about our governments over the years. The selfless sacrifices demanded by a true sense of patriotism take flight in the face of the reality of governments, which over the years have not been able to meet the basic needs of the citizens, but whose leadership has wasted a lot of its resources and lacked the moral authority to rally its citizens to hard work and sacrifices like Lee Kuan Yew did. It was a very difficult lecture, but I did my best. By the third day of training, through series of examples of the modest achievements Nigeria has made in relation to other African countries and through the inspirational appeal that a country is not the same as a government, many acknowledged that their patriotic scale has shifted just a little. It was no longer zero. I enjoyed a momentary triumph. But I was convinced that it would only last momentarily.

As I drove from Kaduna to Abuja after the training, I was reflecting on this experience, and I came to the conclusion that Nigerians are good people, but that over the years of unfulfilled expectations from their governments, they have lost their appetite to make the appropriate sacrifices required for transformation, and have instead acquired values and attitudes that only dwell on the gains of today as they seek an inspirational leader to rally them to greatness. But there is no transformation in history without sacrifice, no transformation without attitudinal change and value reorientation; and no transformation without a very strong work ethic. We all have a role to play drivers, messengers, bricklayers, engineers, doctors, teachers, market women, lawyers, civil servants, political leaders, and, indeed, every citizen. We must change the way we do things.

But it is not only a matter of rhetoric, as was deployed in my training; it is the actions and new orientation of governance, new institutional values, and the nature of incentives and leadership that determine the speed of transformation. In their very popular book, *Why Nations Fail: The Origins of Power, Prosperity and Poverty*[10], Professors Daron Acemoglu and James Robinson argue forcefully that there is no substitute for inclusive economic and political institutions in the journey of transformation. Institutions must be inclusive, not exclusive. In a historical *tour de force*, they showed how nations rose and fell on account of their own actions that denied citizens a stake in their country and its future. In one remarkable example taken from the Kingdom of Kongo, the current Democratic Republic of Congo, it became clear how leadership, choices, incentives, and the absence of inclusive institutions prevented her transformation. The capital of Kongo, Mbaza, had a population of sixty thousand in 1500, about the same size as Lisbon, Portugal, and higher than London at fifty thousand. In a way, Mbaza was developing as a sophisticated capital the same way Lisbon and London were. But that was then. There was early contact with the Portuguese, who brought technology and education to the Kongo. So what happened? Why are they still so poor? The attitude of the leader, the King, was key and the incentives were lacking. According to Acemoglu and Robinson, the citizens "faced a high risk of all their output being expropriated and taxed by the all-powerful king. In fact, it wasn't only their property that was insecure. Their continued existence was hanging by a thread. Many of them were captured and sold as slaves hardly the environment to encourage investment to increase long-term productivity. Neither did the King have incentives to adopt the plough on a large scale or to make increasing agricultural productivity his main priority; exporting slaves was so much more profitable." In this respect, there was one western innovation that the Kongo adopted: the gun, which was required for the capture and export of slaves in response to market incentives.

This is very interesting. Fast forward to today's Nigeria, where many of our leaders are indeed rulers and where our common resources are used for the benefit of few, going by the recent statistics on growing inequality; where poverty has held many of the citizens in servitude; and where corruption not only taxes us excessively, but where high incidences of armed robbery, kidnapping, and terrorism mean that our lives are, once again, being traded for cash. Under these conditions, where is the incentive to deepen or take a strong stake in the nation and its future? How are we different from the Kingdom of Kongo? The only technology we are willing to master is the technology of how to mask the means of our corrupt funds. The incentives we respond to are the ones that provide an immediate reward, irrespective of the means of acquiring them. The only game in town has become politics as a means to an end, defined as taking care of myself, my family, and my unborn, generations. The innovations we embrace are innovations of terror and guns that would enable us to acquire political power and create non-inclusive political and economic institutions. As we struggle for the control of oil wealth, there is no struggle for the competition or control of technology in the oil industry. So that which we own, we do not really own, as we pay and continue to pay heavily to use other people's ideas and technology to bring out the oil. Recall how the PTDF, the institution that was built to enable Nigeria to acquire, master, and dominate oil-related technology, was misused in the recent past. As we debate and adjudicate what the rules for sharing would be in the off-shore/on-shore dichotomy, no one is investing any intellectual capital in what becomes of the nation when there is no oil, or, as we are already witnessing, when nations find their own source of cheap oil or alternative sources of energy. The attitude of dependence on oil means that all the incentives must be provided to ensure its flow, to the detriment of the other productive sectors. The transformation of agriculture along the value chain and the diversification of the economy requires a new understanding, leadership ethos that depart from the old, unproductive attitude and outdated thinking that fail to understand global competitiveness and the role of technology in these sectors. I think that the point has been made. We are not very different from the Kingdom of Kongo in 1500 in terms of institutions, *rulership*, and incentives. So how can the majority have a stake in the country and its future? And no transformation can take place when the majority is powerless.

In their book, The Spirit Level: Why Greater Equality Makes Societies Stronger, Richard Wilkinson and Kate Pickett underscore the importance of inclusiveness and reduced inequality in any transformation agenda. They note that "the transformation of our society is a project in which we all have a shared interest. Greater equality is the gateway to a society capable of improving the quality of life for all of us and an essential step in the development of a sustainable economic system." Greater equality makes for accountable citizenship as society gives voice to the voiceless. In essence, the great inequality we are experiencing in Nigeria must be seen as a hindrance to the transformation agenda, and policies must be targeted at creating greater equality or else the transformation would be at best fragile and, most likely, unsustainable.

It is worth reminding ourselves that the hindrance to a global renaissance is inequality between regions, between nations, and within nations. Renaissance is about the civilisation of our being, which requires us to be socially responsive and to resist the lure or temptation to satisfy individual desires, profligacy, and excessive personal accumulation. Instead, the allure should be towards the creation of what Jeffrey Sachs calls a "mindful society". It is the absence of a mindful society that sees scores of people trying to cross the Mediterranean Sea, with many dying daily and many more trying to escape their dreadful society in spite of the danger. It is the lack of a mindful society that has resulted in a country being ranked as the number one importer of champagne while under-five malnutrition is rampant and polio must be fought with the help of external philanthropy.

In Jeffrey Sachs' elegant and innovative book, *The Price of Civilization: Economics and Ethics, After the Fall,* we are tutored on the several dimensions of a mindful society[11]:

- Mindfulness of self: personal moderation to escape mass consumerism (taking time to understand the source of your own happiness and the importance of collective action)

- Mindfulness of work: the balancing of work and leisure (unemployment is not only a denial of income; it degrades a person, leading to unhappiness and political restiveness)
- Mindfulness of knowledge: the cultivation of education (knowledge of science and expert knowledge is critical for our survival and well-being. This also implies a recognition that specialised skills are required in the management of our economy and that we must govern technology to serve a broad spectrum of society)
- Mindfulness of others: the exercise of compassion and cooperation (government and society must be mindful of the poverty trap and concerned about the many working poor amongst us; the poor status of our public schools, where the poor are trapped without learning, shows a country that is not mindful of the poor. We need to get different communities and ethnicities working together again)
- Mindfulness of nature: the conservation of the world's ecosystems (our response to environmental challenges lacks in-depth knowledge, is short-sighted and we lack adequate institutions for addressing the challenges)
- Mindfulness of the future: the responsibility to save for the future (the absence of a rigorous, consistent national plan and long-term coordinated economic strategy – requires a special will and elite consensus on what the future represents beyond the dictates of short-term political gains)
- Mindfulness of Politics: the cultivation of public deliberation and shared values for collective action through political institutions (the moral imperatives of politics; expertise must be recognised and ignorance avoided; political expedience cannot be allowed to rule. Governments must govern the market and work complementarily for shared prosperity; the internalisation of public debate and public opinion in public policy)
- Mindfulness of the world: the acceptance of diversity as a path to peace (creating trust across national borders, coordinating global efforts against poverty, creating global norms of good behaviour that protect all countries, weak and strong, and promoting common actions that allow all human beings to live in dignity)

CHAPTER THREE

Peace as Justice and Equity

My people are destroyed for lack of knowledge: because thou hast rejected knowledge, I will also reject thee, that thou shalt be no priest to me: seeing thou hast forgotten the law of thy God, I will also forget thy children. – Hosea 4: 6.

Mr. President, Paul Harris Fellows, Distinguished Fellow Rotarians, Ladies, and Gentlemen: It is indeed an honour and a privilege to have been asked to be your guest speaker as we commemorate the 110th anniversary of Rotary International, a celebration that fell into the month in which Rotary is charging us to promote peace and goodwill. I want to salute the courage, selfless service, and dedication of all Rotarians all over the world. Rotary is an example of how one man, Paul Harris, made a difference. And how each one of us in our various vocations can make a difference in our little corners by bringing ethics, "service above self", and love of neighbour, fairness, truth and excellence to bear on what we do or say, in spite of what is happening around us. The United States is not a perfect country now; in 1903, when Paul Harris founded Rotary, it was undoubtedly a broken nation, a bigoted nation in search of its humanity, and it did not stop him. So, my fellow countrymen and women ask not for a perfect country before you act; let's act so that we can have a perfect country. In this charge, I am reminded of the words of President Barack Obama, in his first inauguration address on January 20, 2008:

> He said, 'For they have forgotten what this country has already done; what free men and women can achieve when imagination is joined to common purpose and necessity to courage.

That really is what we have been called to do. To eschew extreme individualism, selfishness, and greed; to use our knowledge, capacity, and wealth for a common purpose; and to dream and conquer all our setbacks for the benefit of all, joining our imagination to a common purpose and working fearlessly to create a brave new world. Paul Harris did it, we too can do it!

Today, I would like to preface my remarks on the subject of peace by referring to and quoting two landmark statements made by two of the world's most remarkable leaders and *intellectual freedom fighters* who, many years ago, were teaching the world the essentials of peace, not only through their selfless leadership and service, but by deconstructing the concept of peace and exposing its true essence. In their many public engagements, they laid bare the critical elements of peaceful co-existence in a diverse world—a world in which we are tied by our common humanity but pulled apart by our political and economic greed and a selfish and jaundiced interpretation of history, religion, identity, nationality, tribe, and race.

> Peace is not the absence of war (tension), but the presence of justice- Dr. Martin Luther King Jr. (In the 1960s).

> Where justice is denied, where poverty is enforced, where ignorance prevails and where any one class is made to feel that society is in organised conspiracy to oppress, rob, and degrade them, neither persons nor property will be safe[12], - Fredrick Douglas, Washington DC, 1886.

From these statements, you can guess where my thoughts are likely to coalesce: that justice, equity, care, love, trust, selfless service, morality in governance, and the promotion of human dignity are at the heart of peace. We promote peace through the service we render to others. Service is not only at the heart of peace; it is what defines and determines it. Service is care; service is love; service is sharing; service is generosity; service is leadership; service is equity; service is justice; and service is trust. Service is what builds understanding and nourishes our common humanity. Just like Harry Truman, the 33rd President of the United States of America, charged Americans and indeed the world several years ago to "build a new world, a far better world—one in which the eternal dignity of man is respected", Rotary is charging Rotarians and indeed all humanity to promote peace and human dignity through the various avenues of service.

And there is no better time for Rotarians and all of us to focus on peace. All around the world, from Asia to Europe, from the Arab world to North America to Africa and Nigeria, inequity and injustice reign, fueling all forms of non-peaceful coexistence and, sometimes, extremist behaviour, often of the violent form. And this is not to excuse violence and extreme behaviour because violence is an unintelligent and incompetent response to social injustice. But it is to recognise how acts of omission or commission that diminish any one's or any group's human dignity: from a rigged election to dictatorship; from corrupt leadership to incompetent or insensitive leadership; from racial to religious bigotry; from human trafficking to modern-day slavery violate the tenets of peace. According to Mahatma Gandhi, "poverty is one of the worst forms of violence". And we have governments that have, over the years, carried on with policies and acts that continually impoverished her people and hoped that all the armies and police of this world would help them maintain peace.

And the Rotary club is right to raise this issue now. With great advances in technology, life is supposed to be more abundant and meaningful for all. With civilization and enlightenment, and with our shared history and common humanity, we are supposed to be more accommodative and tolerant, and we are supposed to have conquered our primordial instincts. Historically, violence was associated with struggles for control of scarce resources. And we still see this struggle in modern times, often disguised, in its most inhuman form as we struggle to define "just and unjust wars". It seems, therefore, that with technology, life has become increasingly more abundant for the few, as those who command this social means of production are increasingly appropriating the massive benefits privately. While technology is promoting interconnectedness and "social intercourse between nations and peoples" through the internet and electronic and social media, it is equally polarising the world as the benefits of the knowledge and technological world are shared unequally. Technology access and control have lost their moral and socialising value.

Sidney Poitier, the great American actor and the first black man to win an Academy Award for best actor, wrote on "faith, love, courage and the future", in his book, *Life Beyond Measure: Letters to My Great Granddaughter*[13], "Before I came into the World, there were challenges, danger, and hunger. I don't know if there was as much hope then, Ayele, as there might appear to be now. By the same token, I can't say that hope now is much more substantive than it was then. I do know that the world as it is today is much more dangerous than it ever was in the past years." And I dare add, a lot more divided and insular than in the recent past.

And indeed, the world is a lot more dangerous now than it has ever been. It is a world where our freedoms as citizens of the world are curtailed by the "non-citizen" actions of kidnappers, armed robbers, cultists, Boko haram members, suicide bombers, and other fringe groups that are equally destroying the basis of their citizenship. It is a world where justice and equity deficits are creating hopelessness and misery, forcing young people to see the state as the enemy and every successful person as an oppressor. But many have been misled to wear the garb of violence in the mistaken belief that it is the means to create hope, justice, and equity. Worse, the guise of violence is increasingly being painted with a new religious paint, with adherents being indoctrinated to see every non-adherent as an enemy and a legitimate target. Therein lays the greater danger. Suddenly, your neighbour and friend becomes targets; your fellow traveler chained by the same yoke of injustice becomes a target; ordinary citizens, passengers on an aircraft, or a group in a church, mosque or market become victims of weapons of mass destruction in the hands of brainwashed religious zealots and used and discarded political miscreants.

It seems, as with all cases of sectarian violence, that perpetrators acting out of ignorance are influenced by an uninformed notion of "singularity of identity" in choosing their targets. Amartya Sen, in his book on identity and violence, argues convincingly that this "singular affiliation syndrome" forces these perpetrators of violence to "ignore altogether all other linkages that could moderate their loyalty… and to ignore all affiliations and loyalties other than those emanating from one restrictive identity and explains how this can be deeply misleading and also contribute to social tension and violence". I am Igbo, a Nigerian, a Christian, a Catholic, a father, a husband, a teacher, a researcher, a banker, an economist, a politician, a Rotarian, and a Paul Harris Fellow. So who am I? How can you target me because I am a Christian or Igbo and ignore my other affiliations, which are equally important. In the community of teachers or Rotarians, where I also belong, there are Christians, Muslims, Hindus, and even atheists; and we enjoy common bonds as teachers and Rotarians. In Nigeria, this identity is taking on new forms: progressives versus non-progressives; resource controllers versus resource de-controllers; littoral states versus non-littoral states; state police advocates versus Federal Police; sovereign conference proponents versus no conference proponents— all with their attendant tensions, threats, and ethnic innuendos.

Because of the diversity of our affiliations, it is illogical to engage in singular identity for the purpose of violence. The plurality of our affiliations makes it nonsensical. Muslims must stop killing Christians, and Christians must stop killing Muslims, because those being killed are Nigerians, fathers, mothers, children, doctors, teachers, businessmen, Rotarians, and human beings. Rotarians in this service year and beyond must use the avenues of service to preach our common bond and heritage and the richness in the multiplicity of our identities. For peace and justice to reign, Rotarians must preach against unbridled and immoral competition, as well as competitive corruption (who can grab the most). In the words of Armatya Sen, "Poverty and economic inequality may not instantly breed terrorism or influence the leaders of terrorist organizations, but they can help to create rich recruiting grounds for the foot soldiers of the terrorist camps." This is worth pondering over as we all must embark on preventive measures whose clear antidote is good governance, which seems to have eluded and continues to elude us with no real consequences for those who have ruled us without leading us. The manifestations of this leadership deficit in society are terrorism, armed robbery, kidnapping, and sexual assault (rape). And the competitive corruption goes on shamelessly. And we know that a nation without shame can hardly make progress.

Within reason, competition for legitimate wealth, competition for recognition, competition for political or economic positions, and even competition for the spread of our faith are all legitimate. What is illegitimate is the uncivil and violent means of staking a position and forcing others to inhumanly surrender to your ambition and interpretation of national, political, and religious affairs, and declaring fellow citizens enemy combatants at the point of execution without first declaring them enemies so that they can protect themselves. Our competition cannot be an all-or-nothing competition. Our competition is supposed to advance us, bring out the best in us, produce the most competent leaders, improve our creativity, and create surplus so that all can share. What we see now is competition based on falsehood; ability has become disability in Nigeria (in the words of a famous politician), and our competition is driven by that limited singular classification and false identity that ignores the plurality of our associations, and we create divisions where none necessarily exists.

Victor E. Frankel describe the "existential vacuum" in his book, *Man's Search for Meaning*[14], as "a wide spread phenomenon of the 20th Century" arising from loss of animal instincts; that paradise of freedom that allows us to label most behavior as arising from instincts. This is coupled with another loss arising from the absence of a dominant culture that prescribes the boundaries of behaviour and determines how we ought to behave. So, we are left unguided, not relying on our primitive instincts, and not bound or disciplined by culture. This would not have been an issue if this phenomenon was benign. But we are now forced to make choices, good or bad, as knowledge beings and enlightened humans. It is this existential vacuum that leads to aggression, suicide, rape, and other off-limit, extreme, and often dangerous behaviours. What have we done to contribute to this existential vacuum that now exists, especially among our youth? It is not simply that we have lost our instincts and dominant culture of control, but that our actions, policies, activities, and personal conduct are creating this existential vacuum for our youth. What hope is there for the future of the youth when teachers do not teach, governors do not govern, ministers do not minister, leaders do not lead, and parents do not parent, and preachers preach hate instead of love? Many of our young people are, therefore, still searching for meaning in their lives.

But more importantly, for the poor and the rich, how are we preparing the young generation, our children, for a life with meaning? The corruption of children, and indeed, society begins in the family. Parents are now paying for someone to take their children's exams or for the invigilator to look the other way or if that fails, to find a way to "fix" the outcome so that their uncompetitive kid would become, at least temporarily, successful. We are flying our kids in business class with public resources while other kids study under the trees. We are raising a generation without character, without love for self and neighbour and without hope, and we are surprised when they indulge in extreme behavior. And I ask, how so? One of my greatest pains in our democratic journey is the use to which our youths are deployed during elections: as election riggers, ballot box snatchers, thugs, and sometimes murderers. And what then becomes of these youths after elections, after they have been used and dumped? Where are love and civility, the fundamentals of a decent society?

And what manner of society, leaders, or rulers do we have? What is their attitude towards democracy – rule by all means?

Where is justice and equity when huge public expenditures have not uplifted the poor, producing growth that is anything but inclusive? Where is justice and equity when governments borrow to consume? And the said consumption is skewed in favour of the wealthy, resulting in one of the world's worst income disparities. Where is the justice and equity when governance has been reduced to road construction with a slew of clueless, sometimes hapless cheerleaders? Can you have equity, and hence peace, in the land when the children of the poor are consigned to educational establishments where there is virtually no learning. If public schools and public health facilities have been abandoned, how would the assets of the poor be improved? How would their productivity, and hence their income, rise? If the children of the poor have no hope of escaping poverty, how can you demand that their parents work hard and be good citizens? If they are not good citizens, the social contract is broken, and the platform for peace to reign is weakened, if not destroyed. You cannot blame them, the young ones, if they begin to nurture a certain self-perception of inadequacy occasioned by alienation from society. It is this self-perception that can easily lead to rigid identities, which, if reinforced by a distinct cultural thrust of being from a particular ethnicity or group, can be a trigger for violence. Unfortunately, education, which gives the power of reasoning that, is required to reverse this self-perception and identity and that is required for greater understanding of other people, is in limited supply and of poor quality. And we observe that sometimes violent expression and other forms of non-citizen behaviour manifest in a lack of courage to confront the pain we all face; in our experience, this lack of courage to live forces the uneducated, the unenlightened, to be trapped in pain and to unleash it on others, mistakenly believing that it will make their pain go away. There is so much that quality education can do to foster peace, justice, and equity. And it is lacking because our rulers have refused to lead. Listen to Lee Kuan Yew, the first Prime Minister of Singapore, in his book from Third World to First: "We are building a nation where everyone has a stake in it now and in its future"[15]. And that is what he has built: a fair nation, a Singapore where everyone has a stake in its prosperity, and he did that using what he called an "honest and effective government".

Let me remind us that the so-called Asia miracle was no miracle. It came because, following Japan, most of these south-east Asian countries laid a solid foundation in education and built the capabilities of their citizens through active public policy and an uncompromising ideology and attitude towards development.

In 1872, a new fundamental code of education was issued in Japan. "There shall, in the future, be no community with an illiterate family; nor family with an illiterate person." Kido Takayoshi, an influential leader of Japan at that time, said: Our people are not different from the Americans or Europeans of today; it is all a matter of education or lack of education."[16] stated that: "By 1910, Japan had, as is generally acknowledged, universal attendance in primary schools. By 1913, even though Japan was still economically very poor and underdeveloped, it had become one of the largest producers of books in the world, publishing more books than Britain and indeed more than twice as many as the United States. Indeed, Japan's entire experience of economic development was, to a great extent, driven by human-capability formation, which included the role of education and training, and this was promoted both by public policy and by a supportive cultural climate... Japan was not only a learner but also a great teacher." In our nation, what do we have? We have a library board library board, full-time staff, and annual budgets, but no library. We have replaced reading with 24-hour Africa Magic viewing through digital television. We have teachers who cannot pass a standardised exam for the class they are supposed to teach. Many families have children in school who cannot read or write. And yet we hope to transform. If you look at the leadership recruitment process, you cannot help but shudder. How can people be expected to give what they don't have? We are engaged in the dance of mediocrity and shame where power is acquired through "stomach infrastructure", a bizarre twist in our democratic journey; where the giver and receiver of this infrastructure demean themselves and the democracy we practice. And it leads me to ask: Are we ready to be governed? More appropriately, when shall we demand good governance and development?

Martin Luther King Jr. said "that power without love is reckless and abusive... and that power at its best is love implementing the demands of justice, and justice at its best is power correcting everything that stands against love." I turned to my religion in search of the true meaning of love. The type of love we should teach our children and neighbours is the type of love that brings peace, as Christ and Prophets of all great religions preached. I can, therefore, not understand how any religion could preach violence or hatred. And I am glad that both Christian and Muslim clerics and scholars agree that Islam and Christianity are religions based on peace and love. Sometime ago, the gospel of our Lord in John 6: 1-15 was the theme of the Catholic homily. In this gospel, Jesus Christ used five loaves and two fish to feed five thousand men. Without going into the details of the exact words of the verses, there are a few actions to note. Note that Christ, the great leader, had empathy for his followers and was concerned enough about their state of well-being to want to feed them. Note further that the five loaves and two fish were volunteered by a small boy in the crowd, an act of selflessness. Note that Christ overruled His disciples, who thought that the situation was hopeless. In preaching the sermon, my bishop used the spirit-inspired interpretation of St. Augustine, who interpreted the two fish as love for God and love for your neighbour. You cannot love for God and your neighbour while engaging in injustice and inequity; you cannot love God and your neighbour while engaging in the kinds of competitive corrupt acts we are all witnessing that have resulted in the harvest of misery for many of our citizens. You will bring hope where there is none, abundance where there is scarcity, joy where there is sadness, and fulfilment where there is emptiness if you love God and neighbour. The huge lessons from this gospel are love, sacrifice, humility in leadership, empathy, selflessness, restoration of human dignity, and inclusiveness.

I want us to end where we started, with the words of Dr. Martin Luther King, Jr. "We must build dikes of courage to hold back the flood of fear… That old law about "an eye for an eye" leaves everyone blind… This time to do the right thing is always right… peace is not merely a distant goal that we seek, but a means by which we arrive at that goal." In fact, it is the means—the indispensable platform—by which all other goals are achieved.

I am an optimist. I know that sooner or later things must change. There is a Turkish proverb that says, "No matter how far you have gone on the wrong road, you can turn back." I hope that we can turn back for the sake of our children and for the sake of this nation. I want to urge us all, as good citizens and people of God, to love God and neighbour through exemplary service, to promote peace through justice and equity, and to go out there and preach this gospel throughout this land and beyond. This is the sure way to underscore our common humanity.

PART TWO
Leadership and National Intergration

CHAPTER FOUR

National Integration, Citizenship and the Challenge of Economic Policymaking[17]

Preamble

Amartya Sen, a Nobel Laureate in economics, argues convincingly in his book, Identity and Violence: The Illusion of Destiny that "singular affiliation syndrome" forces perpetrators of violence and injustice to "ignore altogether all other linkages that could moderate their loyalty… and to ignore all affiliations and loyalties other than those emanating from one restrictive identity …and how this can be deeply delusive and also contribute to social tension and violence". And I dare add inequity and a lack of economic and social progress for the majority.

> We need deeper changes than those on offer today, changes that restore our personal balance and the foundations of our trust in society. We need a mindful society, in which we once again take seriously our well-being, our relations with others, and the operation of our politics…We have become a country of strangers. And that estrangement is accompanied by falling trust. -Jeffrey Sachs

On our common humanity and interdependence, the great Bengali poet, Rabindranath Tagore, stated: [18]"Whatever we understand and enjoy in human products instantly becomes ours, wherever they might have their origin. I am proud of my humanity when I can acknowledge the poets and artists of other countries as my own. Let me feel with unalloyed gladness that all the great glories of man are mine." It follows that skills, talents, and competence have no boundaries, and human progress has relied on knowledge interdependence, highlighting the futility of claims of Western knowledge monopoly.

Introduction

From the selected quotes above, you can easily guess the impetus for this subject and where my thoughts are likely to coalesce. There is no claim to novelty or expertise on this subject on my part, nor do I intend to have the final word on it. Rather, I wish to provoke further intelligent discussions and, hopefully, induce positive, courageous, and enduring action from all of us, from our small spheres of influence, whether as intellectual, political, or economic entrepreneurs.

In examining Nigeria's match towards social and economic progress, it has become very clear that the periods of relative progress have coincided with the period when there was seemingly a convergence on national ideology and when creativity and imagination were brought to bear on a common purpose. It coincided with the times when national leadership had a consensus on the national development agenda, exploited regional strengths and used development plans to establish key industrialization pillars, from steel mills to paper mills, all around the country in a fairly intelligent manner.

The issue of national integration and citizenship rights and how they impinge on our social and economic progress has gained new force because, at a time of unprecedented "national wealth", our match with progress has been stunted. And our fault lines have never been larger or more exposed, nor has citizen alienation higher. Every budget, every appointment, and certain economic policies have an ethnic or regional face—at least Nigerians examine them, unfortunately, through that perception lens. And as we know, perception shapes behaviour, and these behaviours have consequences for our socio-economic progress. Creating a nation where every citizen has a stake in its prosperity and in the burden of creating the commonwealth has become urgent and compelling. Everything else is a distant second.

Ethnicity and National Integration

The natural order of things is to be with, associate with, and construct relationships with people of your kind. The basic human instinct is familia. Many have said that it is part of our DNA. This kind of relationship assumes a natural constriction of the radius of trust, shared values and norms; almost co-integral social protections within the family, as it were. In return, the group enjoys, within the exchange economy, disproportionate gains from the exchange: the assignment of propriety rights and political authority, all of which lead to economic rent that essentially reinforces ethnic identity and forces decisions to be based on ethnic calculations.

What am I saying? That ethnicity is the natural order of things. However, extending this type of relationship, whether manufactured or organic, to the realm of national governance is not only suboptimal; it is anti-development in its very essence. One can analyse every obstacle to Nigeria's development within the framework of the absence of national integration and the contestation among the dominant ethnic groups. Instead of a national "civil public", we have several primordial publics in competition with one another. Healthy competition is useful, but competition for national assets on the basis of ethnic solidarity inevitably retards the socio-economic progress of a nation. How then do you deal with something that, although harmful to national development, seems natural? How can you incentivise a different type of relationship that promotes competence, meritocracy, multiple identities and hence national integration? Can the consciousness of ethnic identity be married with national aspiration and national integration? Can this tribe be enlarged, or is it rigid and narrowing over time? If ethnicity is our reality, in the words of Prof. Claude Ake, can we engineer around it a "more efficient, less traumatic, and less self-destructive social transformation"? Can there be another form of solidarity that promotes national citizenship and, hence, produces enlightened leadership whose economic policies are ethnic or regionally neutral. Why are the common struggles among common people across ethnic lines not enough to withstand the forces that exploit ethnicity for the benefit of the few?

The answer lies in the creation of institutions (credible institutions)—with laws, accepted values, morals, and practises that tie the hands of leaders, provide checks and balances, and incentivise measured achievements. Institutional framework, in the words of Nobel Laureate Douglass North, is responsible for creating the incentive structure of a nation or society, improving its stock of knowledge, and driving economic performance through the "deliberate effort of human beings to control their environment". In his book, *Understanding the Process of Economic Change*[19], Douglas North espouses how the process of social and economic change requires the intentional enactment of institutional change by key policymakers and their comprehension of the issues. He said, "Throughout history and in the present, world economic growth has been episodic because either the players' intentions have not been societal well-being or the players' comprehension of the issues has been so imperfect that the consequences have deviated radically from intention".

I paused as I read this and wondered aloud about our country our country. For nations to make progress, leaders must put citizens at the centre of their policies. Second, capability, competence, and effectiveness must match intentions. It's no use wanting to go to Sokoto when your map, technology and guide are taking you to Yenagoa, or for that matter, when you are incapable of reading the map. You would be making efforts, but you would never get to Sokoto. Have you ever wondered why the more we criminalise corruption, the more corrupt the citizens have become? Have we made the appropriate diagnosis? Is the absence of a sense of nation part of the problem? A problem, perhaps, closely tied to the psychological and emotional distance between the citizens and the Nigerian state.

Our current political system is overly concerned with the region of origin of the office holder and the sponsorship of the office, rather than with prior and measured performance. And we have extended this to a ridiculous extent to how, for instance, the board and governance of parastatals of the government are constituted and managed. If these are serious institutions designed as vehicles for pursuing strategic national policies, why is the tenure of these boards not respected? Why must all boards be sacked, irrespective of performance, because of a regime change and the urge to find jobs for the boys? Can we think of a law that guarantees the tenure of these boards, with the law providing for how their performance can be measured and how they can be sacked?

I read recently the statements credited to President Jonathan as part of his speech at the 50th anniversary celebration of Rivers State concerning Niger Delta Development Corporation (NDDC). He stated that NDDC has not been effective because of frequent changes in its board and management, leading to many abandoned projects as each new management and board starts a new project rather than complete what others started. This is very instructive. Boards of public institutions are not formed to add value but to reward political actors, reflecting the ideology of the leaders in power. And we all know why new management and the board initiate new projects, don't we? *Egunje*! Corruption!

I have a few stories of my own to tell, as they together illustrate our wacky incentive structure, derision for competence and ability, a strong penchant for ethnic proclivity, and how performance, innovation, and citizen welfare are very far from the minds of many policymakers in our land. In 2006, I was the Cabinet Member (Minister) responsible for National Planning. One of the parastatals under National Planning is the foremost research institution in Nigeria, the Nigerian Institute of Social and Economic Research (NISER), based in Ibadan. I met a barely literate Chairman of the Governing Council of NISER and I advised the President to effect a change, incurring the anger of senior policymakers from his area; I advertised the position of the DG of NISER and incurred the wrath (a threatening letter) of a major political player from the city where NISER is located; and a couple of years later, I became the Chairman of a reform-minded Governing Council that was dissolved barely two years after inauguration, even though we had given NISER its first strategic plan. Multiply these experiences, these paralysing attitudes, several times over, and you begin to understand why social and economic change has been difficult and why many with good intentions would soon succumb and become part of the ills of the system.

In the search for national institutions, one may be inclined to turn to political parties. Political parties, if properly constructed, can create new familial relationships based on trust, shared values, common ideology, and a shared understanding of economic and social goals as well as the policies that lead to them. But our political parties have not evolved as credible institutions with a clear agenda driven by an ideology or set of values; rather, they have become a mere platform for the grabbing of power and for entrenching the "our turn, your turn" mentality. Rather than an instrument for national integration and for projecting national idealism, it is an odd bag of ethnic and regional interests—a furnace for sharpening the politics of division. And they often die on account of this lack of common ground that should ordinarily glue them together.

And this is the same infection that ravages the national assembly, where the so-called budget padding is a symptom of the absence of a national focus. While acknowledging that members represent constituencies and should seek to protect certain interests, it is sad to note that there is no consensus on matters of overriding national interest. Basically, there are no national ideological guard rails or overriding philosophies. When the debate came up on how to garner the federal government's support for Lagos as the economic hub of the nation, regional interest rather than national interest forced this issue off the agenda. Yet, we know that Lagos is critical for all Nigerians. The same national spirit is required in pushing for a budget that has some focus on poverty, directing more resources to the region with the greatest need—on a truly needs-based and constituency-demand basis.

National Integration and State-Making

National integration should not be confused with state-making. State-making thrives on force and forges states by pulling national groups together, probably without the consent of the groups, and creating a political community that binds them together. The colonial formation of the Nigerian state is an example of this. The resistance of the state to permitting the exit of groups from the union is also a form of state-making.[20]

But national integration, unlike state-making, which tends to preoccupy Nigeria's dominant national elite, is the deliberate political act of constructing acceptance of the national state in the minds of members of the political community so that they accept the national state both as groups and as individual members. The acceptance is normally based on the confidence that the state fulfills its own side of the social contract while citizens perform their duties and feel a sense of community with other citizens in the polity. This is hard work and requires deliberate and constructive effort. The above conceptualization draws together the ideas of integration expressed by Duverger (1976);[21] and Ake (1967)[22].

The point needs to be made that integration is a matter of degree. But integration becomes an issue when citizens within a political community do not feel a sense of belonging due to denials of rights or privileges of membership. Such rights range from economic to political to socio-cultural and other forms of entitlements that draw from belonging to the political community. The problem of lack of inclusiveness is deepened when a group feels that there is a systematic ploy to bar them from the mainstream of national life. The consequence of this kind of feeling is that the bond of membership among ethnic or other cultural groups is strengthened while patriotism towards the national state is weakened. This development connects the problem of national integration with that of citizenship. In effect, the absence of integration weakens citizenship, and the non-cultivation of the ethos that creates a sense of belonging to the political community causes people to want to opt out.

To place emphasis on national integration without consciously building a democratic citizenship is empty propaganda. In the case of Nigeria, there are fundamental gaps in building democratic citizenship. The idea of democratic citizenship draws in the justice element here. To this end, we can fall back on [23]John Rawls' principles of justice. The first of the two principles is that "each person is to have an equal right to the most extensive scheme of equal basic liberties compatible with a similar scheme of liberties for others. Second: social and economic inequalities are to be arranged so that they are both (a) reasonably expected to be to everyone's advantage and (b) attached to positions and offices open to all" (Rawls, 1971:52). There tends to be a lack of commitment to the above justice principles, upon which state-citizen relationships should be built. Thus, the people are bereft of social protection from the state. The absence of the state paves the way for cultural groups to look after their groups. This strengthens group solidarity among members of a group who feel a stronger bond of membership to such groups than to a nation-state that is unconcerned about their well-being.

The dominant elite are well aware of this. Thus, when they seek support for political positions, they essentially do not feel like persons whose offices require services from the state without recourse to narrow group loyalties. Indeed, they feel like representatives of ethnic groups. Their politics is therefore skewed towards ethnicity. They relegate fairness, equity, justice, and even development to the margins of ethnic interests. They influence job opportunities for the members of their ethnic nationalities; they influence public policy allocation to favour their ethnic groups even if such policies contradict justice and overall national interest.

Underlying many of these difficulties with economic policymaking, including planning, is the absence of a shared vision and sense of nation among the ruling elite. Shared vision allows for credible commitment, which ties the hands of the leaders and allows institutions to deliver on their mandate. Credible commitment requires discipline, sacrifice, and consistency of purpose. Why is the vision of the executive different from that of the legislature? How can you set up a Petroleum Technology Development Fund (PTDF) and allow it to do things other than developing technology for Nigerians to have some control of the oil industry? Why would a regime change abort a national vision or change the mandate of a strategic national institution? How can you plan under undisciplined leadership without a clear national sense of purpose?

A sense of nation implies that a South Eastern leader must see reason and advocate for allocating national resources towards the development of North East because it is in the interest of the nation to do so. Just the same way, a policy to support an automotive industry in the East must receive the support of all rather than be encumbered because policymakers are inefficiently searching for other geopolitical equivalents in order to balance the support to the detriment of the nation. There are affirmative actions that affirm and build a sense of nation, but there are others that destroy it. The entrance scores for various states for federal government colleges illustrate this. It discriminates not on the basis of state of residence but on the basis of state of origin, even if the two children were born in the same locality under the same circumstances.

In development planning, we must recognise our sectoral and regional strengths and weaknesses and build on them in order to deal with our weaknesses, realising they are our common strengths and weaknesses. In Nigeria, the prism of assessment or consideration is, for the most part, not Nigeria, not common purpose; our imagination is tied to other parochial considerations.

In April 2012, I published a widely circulated article in several major Nigerian newspapers titled: The Reality of the North-South Divide: Why Jonathan should appoint a National Coordinator for the North. The premise of this article is that we are one nation and plan to remain so in whatever form it takes. And there are very important reasons for reexamining the current form. I was making the point that available statistics show glaring and significant differences between the South and the North and that this gap is not healthy for the nation. My point was that this was not a northern problem but a national problem that required a national solution. The essence of the office of the National Coordinator was to begin the debate, place all the debilitating factors on the table, and create the platform for the articulation of a national response in the interest of all Nigerians. Unfortunately, this argument did not gain traction. Recently, Mallam Sanusi, the Emir of Kano, has returned to this issue of the North-South divide. It is central to the question of national integration and our aspiration for a united, democratic, and prosperous nation. Once again, I would urge that we have a national dialogue on this matter as a serious signpost that we are serious about creating a political community that cares. I must admit that at this time, when the basis of the unity of the country is being debated, with new arrangements being proposed, this proposal will still not gain the desired traction.

Citizenship and Economic Policymaking

In their rhetoric, Nigerian political actors and policymakers pretend that citizens are at the centre of political activities and decision-making. This pretext is hollow because, in the process of acquiring political power, citizenship is merchandised through money for votes and other unwholesome trade-offs, which in turn lead to the vacation of citizenship responsibility and the drowning of their voices. It is, therefore, not a matter of political rhetoric because that is cheap. It is the actions and new orientation of governance, new institutional values; and the nature of incentives and leadership that create citizen-centered economic policies, which in turn determine the speed of transformation of any nation.

There is a state-citizen disconnect in Nigeria. The calls in recent times for the restructuring of the state are important indicators of that disjuncture (see Nigerian Tribune, July 24, 2016; Thisday, June 12, 2016; Vanguard, May 13, 2017; Vanguard, March 31, 2017). The basic idea is that the nature of value allocation in the state is a source of national tension and needs to be reorganised for groups to feel properly integrated into the polity and with one another. Thus, the entire idea of restructuring could be grounded on citizenship and its corresponding rights. Once these rights are addressed, restructuring will have been completed.

The absence of citizenship rights underscores the concerns of many that our leaders, indeed, rulers, are using our common resources for the benefit of a few. The recent statistics on growing inequality buttress this point (the recent Oxfam report is very damning—the combined wealth of the 6 richest Nigerians can wipe out poverty in the land). The nature of value allocation in Nigeria has created a situation where poverty has held many of the citizens in servitude; where corruption not only taxes us excessively, but high incidences of armed robbery, kidnapping, and terrorism mean that our lives are, once again, being traded for cash. Under these conditions, where is the incentive for citizens to deepen or take a strong stake in the nation and its future? How are we different from the Kingdom of Kongo? The only technology we are willing to master is the technology of how to mask the means of our corrupt funds. The incentives we respond to are the ones that provide an immediate reward, irrespective of the means of acquiring them. Politics has become the only game in town as a means to an end, defined as taking care of myself, my family, and future generations. The innovations we embrace are innovations of terror and guns that would enable us to acquire political power and to create and appropriate non-inclusive political and economic institutions. As we struggle for the control of oil wealth, there is no struggle for the competition to build or control the technology used in the oil industry. So that which we own, we do not really own as we pay and continue to pay heavily to use other people's ideas and technology to bring out the oil. Recall how the PTDF, the institution that was built to enable Nigeria to acquire, master, and dominate oil-related technology, was misused in the recent past. As we debate and adjudicate what the rules for sharing would be in the off-shore/on-shore dichotomy, no one is investing any intellectual capital in what becomes of the nation when there is no oil, or, as we are already witnessing, when nations find their own source of cheap oil or alternative sources of energy. The attitude of dependence on oil means that all the incentives must be provided to ensure its flow to the detriment of the other productive sectors. I think that the point has been made. In terms of institutions, *rulership*, and incentives, we are not dissimilar to the Kingdom of Kongo in 1500. So, how can the majority have a say in the country's future? And no transformation can take place when the majority is powerless.

Robert Reich, has taught us that "inequality undermines the trust, solidarity, and mutuality on which the responsibilities of citizenship depend."[24] As a result, it is not a trivial matter. When people are robbed of the dignity that stable employment provides, we all run the risk of feeling insecure. If our leaders are not creating an inclusive, compassionate society, we will court restiveness. If we are not creating a country according to Lee Kuan Yew, where "everyone has a stake now and in its future", we cannot get the commitment of citizens, democratic citizens, now, and the inequality in the future would certainly widen.

It is such inequality that should be the target of public policies, especially economic policies. The instrument of economic policy is the channel of intervention that addresses the material dimension of citizenship. According to Marshall (1950), such intervention is expected to not only elevate the citizen to the status of a civilised being, but also influence his or her subjective feeling that the polity cares and, for that matter, is a source of pride that should be associated with. To illustrate, we draw from the history of the decline of the Roman Empire, which, among other factors, was linked with the decline in the state's attitudes towards its citizens. By the early fifth century, just before the fall of Rome, property rights as well as the economic and political rights of the citizens had declined. These citizenship rights and other privileges, which were prevalent in republican Rome and ensured economic prosperity, had been squandered. Whatever power the citizens exercised had been taken away from them. In accounting for this development, Acemoglu and Robinson (2013) recorded that when the Roman Empire evolved institutions that were extractive, psychological approbation of the state waned among the citizens. This development affected the economic growth of Rome, the morale of the Roman army, and the citizens' support for the state. It was this fault line that undermined the great empire before the decline was completed by the military victory of its conquerors.

The Dilemma of Development Planning In the Absence of Shared Vision

Underlying many of these difficulties with planning is the absence of shared vision and a sense of nation among the ruling elite. Shared vision allows for credible commitment, which ties the hands of the leaders and allows institutions to deliver on their mandate. Credible commitment requires discipline, sacrifice, and consistency of purpose. Why is the vision of the executive different from that of the legislature? How can you set up a Petroleum Technology Development Fund (PTDF) and allow it to do things other than develop technology for Nigerians to have some control of the oil industry? Why would a regime change abort a national vision or change the mandate of a strategic national institution? How can you plan under undisciplined leadership without a clear national sense of purpose or the right attitude for transformation?

A sense of nation implies that a South Eastern leader must see reason and advocate that we need to put national resources towards the development of North East because it is in the interest of the nation to do so. Just the same way, a policy to support an automotive industry in the east must receive the support of all rather than be encumbered because policymakers are inefficiently searching for other geopolitical equivalents in order to balance the support to the detriment of the nation. There are affirmative actions that affirm and build a sense of nation, but there are others that destroy it. In development planning, we must recognise our sectoral and regional strengths and weaknesses and build on them in order to deal with our weaknesses, realising that they are our common strengths and weaknesses. In Nigeria, the prism of assessment or consideration is, for the most part, not Nigeria, not common purpose; our imagination is tied to other parochial considerations.

In his 2012 State of the Union address, President Barack Obama stated that "it is public research dollars, over the course of 30 years, that helped develop technologies to extract all this natural gas out of shale rock…government support is critical in helping businesses get new energy ideas off the ground". Here, President Obama was acknowledging that the United States is a developmental state: its federal government uses public resources in a smart way—support for research—to support and subsidise private initiative in pursuit of industrial policy by other means. He revealed the consistency of the Federal government in pursuing a strategic goal, irrespective of the party in power. He further revealed the credible commitment that allows institutions to rise above politics and stay on course with their mandate. Obama's statement demonstrated that even though there is no national planning agency, there is a plan, a multi-year plan, to help actualise a vision. In this case, the planning for the development of a technology that cracked open the shale rock for oil and gas took 30 years of investment. It is the same determination and planning that led to the translation of President Kennedy's vision in 1962 that Americans would land someone on the moon into reality in 1969.

It is important to note that in 1982, when the Federal government started the investment Obama referred to, he was 21 years old and an undergraduate. Since 1982, you've had three Republican presidents and two Democratic presidents. But the investment in the search for this technology was uninterrupted. It is equally worthy of note that while the Federal government was investing, it was clear that some states where the shale rock deposit exists would benefit more than the others, but that did not deter the various governments from funding the research. No one argued against this investment because the territory that would benefit most did not vote for the party in power. [25]

In 1982, when Dr. Mahathir Mohamad was running for the election that would make him the Prime Minister of Malaysia, he chose the slogan: clean, efficient, and trustworthy. In his memoir, A Doctor in the House, he said that he knew that Malays disliked change. But he knew that Malaysia would not develop if they stuck to their old ways. According to him, [26]"I always believed that things could be done differently and that value systems determine the success or otherwise of an individual, a community, or a nation. While the values of a community or nation develop naturally, they can also be deliberately inculcated, and the best way to do this is for the government to practise these values." He set up a plan to clean up corruption and promote efficiency and trustworthiness. In explaining why nations fail, distinguished economists Acemoglu and Robinson, noted that "the extent to which people trust each other and cooperate is important" as products of their institutions and politics. What was the result of Malaysia's campaign to clean-up corruption? According to the Prime Minister, the Customs Department was efficient in collecting monies due to the government; in his words, "government has always had enough money to pay salaries and the cost of development projects without borrowing. We were also always able to tide over financial crises that came our way because we were financially strong. Most other countries would not have been able to do what we did."

In order to create a sense of shared vision and fair distribution of prosperity in Malaysia, a new economic policy was formulated in 1971. Essentially, the government realised that if most Malays were excluded from the mainstream economy, as was the case prior to the implementation of the new economic policy, the country would not make much progress. Malaysia is a multi-ethnic country with a majority of Malays and a minority of Chinese and Indians. In part by resolving what Dr. Mahatir Mohamad referred to as the "Malay Dilemma", the New Economic Policy sought to give every ethnic group a sense of belonging and a stake in their country, then and in the prosperity of her future. This economic affirmative action created the peace and elite consensus required to plan for the orderly development of their country on their own terms. Today, Malays operate in every strata of the Malaysian economy as mechanics, business owners, and chief executives of companies through a deliberate policy that suits their circumstances. But this was still a work in progress.

In 1991, the idea of a long-term plan occurred to the leadership of Malaysia, and they turned to the Institute of Strategic and International Studies (ISIS) to develop a conceptual blueprint that articulated their social, economic, and political paths—a 30-year plan dubbed Vision 2020 which outlined what Malaysia needed to do to be a developed country. The target was a USD 16, 000 per capita incomes and an average growth rate of seven percent for the 30-year period.

In the consultation and launch that followed this vision 2020, the Prime Minister indicated that he would, in his words, "first establish a single, united Malaysian nation." He said, "Though born of different races, all Malaysians had to see themselves as nationals of one and the same country. Different though we were in our origins, ours was a common destiny. We might also differ politically, but our loyalty and dedication to the nation had to be unshakeable. We were all, without reservation or limitation, part of *Bangsa Malaysia* – a single Malaysian people, unified yet diverse – a Malaysia where you are free to express your historical identity but not in a separatist form." And he said something else that is very important. He wanted "Malaysia to develop and be modern according to our own historic pattern with our own distinct ethical and moral values intact—not by aping others and losing our soul."[27] When economists advise on economic reforms in the abstract and idealistic sense, what costs do they assign to national integration and nation building? Or for that matter to regime survival in a fragile polity?

The Vision 2020 provided a platform for planning, intelligent risk-taking, investing in research, innovation and changing the mindset of immediate return by realising that the product of research takes a long time to materialise. In 2016, Malaysia launched its 11th five-year plan (2016 -2020) aimed at transforming itself into an advanced country by 2020. Her current per capita income is USD 11,371 and that of Nigeria is USD 2,085, with a life expectancy of 76 years as opposed to 55 years in Nigeria. This is a country that Nigeria was way ahead of at independence. Today, Nigeria is sending our engineering students on scholarship to Malaysian universities.

We turn to China to illustrate a sense of shared vision and how to build on regional advantages. China has three city groups as economic growth poles: the Yangtze River Delta centred on Shanghai; the Pearl River Delta, centred on the cities of Guangzhou and Shenzhen, and the Jing-jin-yi, centred on Tianjin. A fourth is being planned. According to Chinese Scholars, Lin Ling and Liu Shi-Quin of the Sichuan Academy of Sciences, China's development strategy prioritised the development of the eastern region, which contains these three growth poles. The decision to start from the east was predicated on the unique territorial advantages of the east. But these Eastern growth poles, according to these academics, have made great contributions to the economic and social development of China. They contribute more than 41 percent of all economic aggregates in China. The fourth pole was planned in the West, the Chengdu-Chongqing Zone, aimed at forming a network with the three earlier zones in the East and intended to achieve a balanced and coordinated regional development around the country.[28] In the 12th national development plan of China (2011-2015), the development of Western China was clearly stated as a goal. In addition to the other goals of developing 7 priority industries, inclusive growth, increasing domestic consumption, improve energy efficiency, move into high-end manufacturing, improving the lives of ordinary Chinese and reduction in income inequality.[29] The lessons are clear: an effective development plan must build on the territorial advantages of each region. You cannot create these advantages where they do not initially exist. But for a balanced, inclusive and coordinated development, the return on the investment in the advantaged region can be used to plan and create other economic growth poles. This kind of planning requires strong leadership, a broad mindset, a sense of shared vision and commitment to long-term planning.

The reason why the world is interested in the Chinese plan is that there is elite consensus around the plan, and from experience, the plan has in-built credibility that would guide the policy direction of China for the next five years.

CHAPTER FIVE

The Lateef Jakande Phenomenon: Public Housing, Lessons in Leadership, and Leadership Recruitment

This is truly a phenomenon because this seemingly simple act is not simple at all. If it were, why are there no other true followers who have replicated this feat?

Being human must be the ethical yardstick for all Economic (and Social) Actions– Hans Kung

I feel greatly honoured and humbled to be asked to give this lecture in honour of an iconic leader, a true Awoist, a quintessential journalist, a man who truly placed "service above self", who tackled difficult assignments with courage and efficiency, and who gave the common man a stake in the affairs of this nation. When I was asked by the organisers of this conference whether I was willing to accept this assignment, I did not dither. I quickly rearranged my travel plans and returned to the country on the 18th of November to be here today. But what choice do I have? Those who invited me are people I greatly respect and the subject matter of the lecture – Pa Jakande- is someone I have held in awe since I was a fresh university graduate in 1979, when he distinguished himself as a competent, visionary, and empathetic governor of Lagos State who championed for the world to see how public service and imagination can be used for common purpose in the provision of housing for the lower echelon of the society in what can easily be described as the Jakande phenomenon. This is truly a phenomenon because this seemingly simple act is not simple at all. If it were, why are there no other true followers who have replicated this feat? The efforts of our few true heroes should not be in vain now. They should be rewarded while they are alive, and we as a people and the government must change the culture of recognising deserving leaders and naming monuments after them posthumously. This celebration of one of our heroes who epitomised honesty, integrity, and simplicity is, indeed, very timely at a time when the nation is in search of transformative leaders as we engage in a constant struggle and futile effort of trying to convert rulers to leaders in an era of *rulership* rascality, where incompetence and dishonesty are rewarded and a N30 (8 cents of a dollar) Naira meal has become a benchmark for good living and a measure of a hunger-free Nigeria.

A look at global statistics clearly reveals that the more inclusive and democratic a country is, the lower the number of its citizens without adequate housing. Bear with me; the statistics are reported in different forms. Ghana has 5.5 million people living in slums (about 19 per cent of her population); in Guinea, 43 per cent, Cote d'Ivoire (56 percent), Liberia (67 per cent), Namibia, 34 per cent of the population live in slums. The same source states that Nigeria has 24.4 million Nigerians who were homeless with over 70 percent of Lagosians living in informal housing. When you turn to Europe and America, the picture is very different. England has 59,110; Finland (7112); Norway (3909); Croatia (2000); Belgium (3386); Ireland (9104); and the United States (553,700).[30] We are therefore faced with a global challenge, but the housing crisis is much more daunting in Africa and Nigeria, and the crisis is made worse because there is no concerted leadership attention to addressing this significant social problem. As a result, the focus of this chapter is not on housing per se, but on the leadership required to mobilise intellectual capital and political will in addressing and prioritising this critical human need. Pa Lateef Jakande exemplifies that exceptional leadership by bridging the housing supply deficit like no other leader in our country.

In the Federalist Papers No. 62, James Madison, the fourth American President and one of the main architects of the American Constitution, wrote in 1778 that "a good government implies two things: first, fidelity to the object of governance, which is the happiness of the people; and second, a knowledge of the means by which that object can be best obtained." Further interpretation of this will yield that a government must be devoted, passionate, and unequivocally committed to the happiness of all the people—that is the goal; that is the raison d'être for government, and the only reason why someone would want to enter politics to lead his or her people. The second leg of James Madison's statement implies that those whose responsibility it is to achieve this goal must be competence and character; that their word is their bond; that the content of their policies and implementation of these policies must bear fidelity, true allegiance, to the happiness of the people; and that the structure of governance must be pragmatic, creative, and intelligent in order to support good governance for the delivery of happiness to the people. And there is more. There must be the political will—the courage and determination to change things from what they are to what they ought to be – and the ability and willingness to deal with difficult economic, social, and political issues in the overall national interest, irrespective of the costs to your immediate, narrow constituency. The absence of this political will undermines not only the "fidelity to the object of governance" – the happiness of all the people—but also the "knowledge of the means" of attaining the lofty goal. As an aside, I would suggest that those who are pushing the argument for restructuring the nation, which I think makes a lot of sense, should construct their arguments in terms of the means for generating greater happiness for the generality of our people. Can happiness for the people come from the current constitution and the structure we have? Please note that while the calculus of happiness may differ, happiness knows no tribe, no ethnicity, no nationality, and no religion. It is the product of one's interactions with the socio-economic, political, and legal ecosystem in which one finds oneself. This ecosystem depends on the state, its leadership, and the attitude they bring to governance. And there is more to be said here. But it is not the subject of this chapter.

Let us examine the Jakande phenomenon—the provision of decent low-cost housing for Lagosians—against this background. The market is capable of resolving the housing shortage for the rich with little government intervention. The difficult part is in the provision of decent and affordable housing for the middle and lower echelons of society. But leaders are elected to tackle difficult problems with courage and efficiency. In true Madisonian leadership, Pa Jakande confronted this issue head-on, and it became the sign-post for his very eventful regime as the governor of Lagos State. I wasn't there, but I am almost certain that many in his circle thought he was embarking on an impossible task with little political value—especially in our clime where the elite or godfathers determine the outcome of political contests and where performance and merit are at the bottom of the criteria for the selection of candidates for political office. For those who doubted Pa Jakande or his courage to take-on difficult tasks, I am reminded of the words of President Barack Obama, in his first inauguration address on January 20, 2008, as he set out his policies to renew the American economy and his admonition to his countrymen and women to reflect on the achievements of their heroes when "imagination is joined to common purpose, and necessity to courage". Currently in Nigeria, we see imagination mingled with greed and avarice, and courage taking flight in the face of extreme necessity, where courage is more often than not mingled with impunity.

The land use decree of 1972, which gave trusteeship of all land in the state to the government of the state, nay, the governor, envisaged that the land would be used to pursue the goal of happiness for all. With public land, public housing becomes feasible. The provision of one of the three cardinal needs of man, shelter, is one of the strongest ways of ensuring happiness for all. But what have we been doing recently? We have privatised the public lands, and, in many instances, have auctioned them to the highest bidder in pursuit of happiness for a few. Where there is Banana Island for the rich, is there consideration for an Orange Island or even an Egbalumo Island for the lower echelon of society? This seems to be the new policy thrust.

This is not what Pa Jakande did. A man born on July 29, 1929, who was recruited and encouraged to enter politics by Pa Awolowo and who understood progressive politics devoted his life to serving the people of Lagos. Pa Jakande's government constructed over 30,000 housing units, including low-cost housing estates in Amuwo-Odofin, Ijaiye, Dolphin, Oke-Afa, Ije, Abesan, Iponri, Ipaja, Abule Nla, Epe, Anikantamo, Sululere, Iba, Ikorodu, and Badagary. To fund this gigantic project, the Jakande government increased the tenement rates and price of plots of land in the affluent areas of Victoria Island and Lekki Peninsula. And he did something really smart: he increased the processing fees for lottery, pools, and gaming licenses. This act and his achievements in the housing sector are unmatched.

This is classical Madisonian. Pa Jakande kept fidelity to the object of government and delivered happiness to the people of Lagos, especially the less-privileged. And there is no greater means of delivering happiness than to make someone the owner of a piece of real estate. And what was more; he devised an intelligent and egalitarian means of addressing this very important object of government—taxing the rich to socialise the wealth of a nation and bridge inequality. This is how to create a "mindful society".

It is worth reminding ourselves that the hindrance to a global renaissance is inequality between regions, between nations, and within nations. Renaissance is about the civilization of our being, which requires us to be socially responsive and to resist the lure or temptation to satisfy individual desires and profligacy. and excessive personal accumulation. Instead, the allure should be to build a compassionate society.

But a caring society can only be created by what the distinguished Nobel Prize-winning economist, Arthur Lewis, referred to as an intelligent government, the sort of purposeful and focused government Pa Jakande and his team represented. The government of Pa Jakande combined these two critical elements of a mindful society in constructing his social policies in housing and education and triumphed beyond expectations. The footprints of this success are in full glare for all to appreciate. The triumph of ignorance and the anti-intellectual stance of many of our governments at all levels have not allowed us to tap into the rich intellectual capital within our shores and in the diaspora to resolve our many economic and social issues. It has also blinded us to the fact that compassion and empathy for the poor are signs of strength, not weakness, for our common humanity is as weak as our weakest link. Pa Jakande was indeed the champion of a "mindful society" of our time.

Do you know what the current betting and lottery revenues in Lagos can do for low-cost housing in Lagos? Lotteries and betting companies are typically patronised by low-income individuals. Would it not make sense that this (sin) money is used to do good for them?

Housing, Citizenship and Social Capital

Housing is more than shelter. It confers dignity, social acceptability, protection from social risks, and convening power; it engenders social inclusion, social peace, etc. When this is understood, the benefit of housing extends beyond the individual to the entire society. As a result, it stands to reason that housing policy is at the heart of the government's social policy. Whether it is protection from social risks, mitigating labour market uncertainties, increasing primary school enrollment, or strengthening national orientation and citizenship, access to housing is critical. Banditry, kidnapping, *area boys'* thuggery, and other forms of criminality are, in part, associated with lack of access to decent housing and a fixed abode. And this is why all democratic and progressive governments are concerned about housing supply in terms of affordability and quality for all segments of society. In many countries, it has become an issue of social rights, and social housing (public housing provision policy) is used to craft socially acceptable behaviour.

It is important to understand that accountable citizenship is driven by education, a sense of belonging, and inclusion: equality before the law and equitable access to social services, including housing. Please also note that a socially progressive housing policy bridges inequality. And there is no greater impetus for responsible citizenship than a more equal society. In essence, the great inequality we are experiencing in Nigeria must be seen as a hindrance to our democracy, and to our economic and social progress. But guess what? The inequality of today would pale in comparison to the inequality of the future. Even if we succeed in using technological advances to raise productivity, leading to a bigger economic pie, differential access to the pie would widen. Access to this pie would be determined by how prepared the citizens are. And the children of the rich are increasingly better prepared than the children of the poor. This is why significant intellectual capital must be devoted to crafting and implementing creative social policies that address the access of the poor to the bigger pie when it materialises.

Two nations, the United States of America and Singapore, which are very different in many ways, recognised the importance of housing provision in creating "a mindful society". Capitalism (the market economy), by definition, breeds inequality, and social policies are crafted as a means of ameliorating this deleterious effect. These countries are far from perfect examples. But I am using them to illustrate what focused leadership and state action can do to build citizenship and a sense of belonging among the populace.

President Franklin D. Roosevelt, the 32nd President of the United States and a progressive democrat from Georgia, led the fight for fair and equitable housing access in America. It was a fight because, at his time, a socially progressive policy like low-income housing was considered a socialist idea. Landlords and real estate developers felt that the rental and sales markets would be undercut by cheap public housing. Congressmen with a conservative bent felt that such a programme would create an unmanageable budgetary bulge, while those from rural communities felt that such housing programmes would have an inevitable urban bias and would therefore disadvantage their constituencies. But the President and like-minded Senators like Senator Wagner persisted. His persistence, his vision of a fair and equitable society, and his deployment of huge intellectual capital (knowledge of the means) converted many in the Congress and led to the Housing Act in September 1937. President Roosevelt, in his State of the Union Address of January 6, 1937, spoke on the urgent need to address the housing situation in the country. He said:

> There are far-reaching problems still with us for which democracy must find solutions if it is to consider itself successful. For example, many millions of Americans still live in habitations that not only fail to provide the physical benefits of modern civilisation but also breed disease and impact the health of future generations. The menace exists not only in the slum areas of very large cities but in many smaller cities as well. It exists on tens of thousands of farms, in varying degrees, in every part of the country.[31]

In his second inaugural address, he continued to make the same points. He said:

> I see one-third of a nation ill-housed, ill-clad, and ill nourished. The test of our progress is not whether we add more to the abundance of those who have much; it is whether we provide enough for those who have too little.

To President Roosevelt, access to adequate housing is not simply a need but a right, and he included "the right of every family to a decent home" in the second bill of rights. He asserted that political rights were inadequate for assuring Americans equality in the pursuit of happiness. He said that "necessitous men are not free men" – people without jobs, food, or housing cannot be expected to exercise the responsibilities of citizenship. It is the absence of these freedoms that undermines democracy and breeds dictatorship. If these issues are not addressed in Nigeria, her democracy would be compromised. We are beginning to see some semblance of this. Democracy is incompatible with joblessness, illiteracy, homelessness, and hunger. A voting card in the hands of a hungry, homeless person is dangerous and subject to abuse. No wonder people are willing to sell this democratic right for a pot of porridge or simply block their reasoning and make wrong political choices over and over. But can you really blame them? They don't feel like part of society.

The Housing Act of 1937 established public housing programmes to enable housing agencies all over America to provide decent, safe, and sanitary housing for low-income families. In this act, Congress authorised the federal government to issue bonds to finance the development of new public housing. Through the United States Housing Agency (USHA), about USD 500 million was made available as loans for low-cost housing across the country, with USHA acting as a loan granting agency to the States at a very low interest rate and for a tenure of up to 60 years. In three years, over 500 projects were on-going with about 90 per cent completion.

The success of this programme propelled President Lyndon B. Johnson to upgrade it by establishing Housing and Urban Development as a full ministry of the federal government in 1965. The act required HUD to provide housing, urban, and community development assistance, as well as to ensure that everyone has access to "fair and equal housing". It operates through a network of 2600 state, regional, and local housing agencies in order to address the needs of eligible grantees. HUD has a Capital Fund provided for annually in the budget of the United States. In addition to making grants to the housing agencies, the fund can be used in cases of emergencies where the president has not declared a national disaster and in cases of security and safety emergencies. To emphasise the importance of housing in her social policies, a portion of the capital fund is dedicated to education and training in community facilities—to provide early childhood education, adult education, job retraining (building confidence and networking capacities), and social capital for public housing residents. There are huge lessons for Nigeria in terms of the relationship between the Federal and State governments in this important sector and how the different housing delivery institutions can be coordinated for effective delivery of low-cost housing in

Nigeria. Unfortunately, the sort of leadership attitude we saw in America and that was exemplified by Pa Jakande is lacking in this respect. There is a strong retreat and a lack of impetus in addressing this extremely pressing need.

To understand the housing or social policy of Singapore, you have to appreciate the mentality, attitude, and sense of urgency of her leadership. Prime Minister Lee Kuan Yew led the transformation of Singapore, from poverty to prosperity in three decades. It was underpinned by an attitude that was informed by his "hatred for cruelties on fellow Asians" by the Japanese; his sense of "nationalism and self-respect", his "resentment at being lorded over"; his sense of confidence; his abhorrence for an environment that bullied the Chinese minority; his willingness to rally Singaporeans to the "hardship of going it alone"; and his determination to "build a multi-racial society that would give equality to all citizens". It was an attitude of "hard work, planning, and improvising." As far as the leaders were concerned, an honest, effective, and democratically elected government was required for ensuring security, social and economic progress. Implying a government whose attitudes and aspirations must reflect the citizens, the informed and patriotic electorate. It means a work force imbued with positive values, willing to give its best, and managed for greater productivity.

Now that we have briefly reviewed the philosophy and the broad guiding ethos of the leadership of Singapore, let us briefly examine how their distinct housing policy was at the centre of creating a nation "where everyone has a stake in it now and in its future". Both in terms of scale, quality, and delivery pattern, Singapore's housing policy is unique. About 80 per cent of Singapore's citizens live in the flats built by the Housing and Development Board through a policy that combines private and public actions. The houses are built by the government and sold to the public on a 99 year lease. These houses can be sold later in secondary markets. Rather than rental, the emphasis of social housing in Singapore is on ownership. The second pillar of Singapore's social housing is to situate it within the context of social security: to mitigate labour market uncertainties and the absence of robust unemployment benefits, subsidised housing becomes the main source for maintaining social peace and a healthy citizenship since housing expenditure is often the largest share of household expenditures. The third is that housing was used as a means of encouraging high-level saving during active working years and for old-age sustenance through a reverse mortgage. Under a central provident fund, workers contributed 20 percent of their salaries, while employers contributed 17 per cent. This was initially meant as a retirement fund, but the rules were changed to allow for the fund to be used to buy houses. The central provident fund became essentially a housing savings scheme with a provision that the equity in the house should be released upon retirement. It is these savings that the government targets by issuing a bond to the central provident fund. The government uses the fund to finance public housing through loans and grants to the Housing Board. The Board sells the flats to the public and gives them loans to help them pay for them. These loans are repaid from further CPF savings. In addition, the government makes grants to some first-time buyers.

There is even more. Housing was used for other forms of social engineering and building social capital: encouraging certain household forms, encouraging ethnic mix, networking through community activities, promoting healthy living through recreational and sports activities embedded in the public housing plan, and serving as social hubs for accessing other social services. Eligibility, priority, and subsidy depend on income, marital status, and age.

Finally, "public housing in Singapore was the pillar of an asset-based social development that redistributed incomes across the individual's life stages, from working years to retirement years, rather than between income groups in society"[32]

Our pension reform was thoughtful and courageous. It has advanced the pension scheme from an archaic and broken system to a more sustainable and predictable one. It required strong leadership. However, unlike Singapore, we have not tapped into large pension funds for finance housing. We need to reform the pension scheme so that it can support low-income social housing in a way that is delivers both quality and affordability. The federal government should work with state housing and urban development agencies to promote universal homeownership and urban renewal. I have always argued that in a federation, the role of the federal government is to provide competitive support to the states to address infrastructure gaps. The Lagos Metro project that Pa Jakande conceived should have been a joint project of Lagos State and the Federal Government. Such a project should never be entangled in unnecessary political wrangling.

Pa Jakande and the Leadership Recruitment Process

It is important to examine the leadership recruitment process that threw-up Pa Jakande as the Governor of Lagos State in 1979. This is crucial in understanding his fidelity to the object of government–the provision of happiness for the populace, especially the weaker segment of society. Part of the crisis of leadership in Nigeria is the opportunistic, often mercantile nature of our current leadership recruitment process. Leaders, in the words of the leadership scholar Maxwell, are "those who see before others see and see farther than they see …and they are people with true influence." But to be visionary and transformative, a leader must have knowledge, character, experience (relevant experience), exposure, and intuition; she must know what she doesn't know and be constantly in a learning mode. Today, Nigeria's greatest natural enemy is itself, because all its problems, including leadership failure, are caused by human choice. In the words of Joshua Greene in his book, *Moral Tribes*[33], "we face the tragedy of common-sense morality: moral tribes that can't agree on what's right or wrong." I don't know whether we are a moral tribe or not, but I know that we are tending towards a tragedy of common sense immorality—there is a consistency in making wrong choices and lamenting over the outcomes time and again. Unfortunately, this is beginning to breed democratic tyranny and undermine our democracy.

In an inaugural lecture I delivered in April 2018 at the University of Nigeria Nsukka on "WHY ARE THEY SO POOR?" I stated that "poor nations are poor because competent and visionary leadership has eluded them. Unfortunately, poverty reinforces the entrenchment of mediocre leadership in a seemingly unending cycle. Development occurs when leaders with the right attitude emerge and make choices that are underpinned by honesty, hard work, and efficiency. [34]In his memoir, Le Kuan Yew[35] further emphasised the importance of the quality of political actors and top government officials. Therefore, in his own words, he "set out to recruit the best into government", not leaving leadership to chance or allowing the politics of Singapore to be dominated by what he called "political activists". [36] We must ask ourselves, what is the leadership recruitment process in Africa and in this country? How can you plan in an environment dominated by those who do not see tomorrow? Lee Kuan Yew understood that you cannot give what you don't have. In what has been appropriated by lawyers, the Latin recognised that "*nemodat quod non habet*" which the French acknowledges as "*personne ne peut donne cequ'il n' a pas*. It is a settled matter; you cannot give what you don't have.

But in the leadership lexicon of Nigeria, money is what determines who becomes a "leader". In Igbo, they will say that "*onye bu igu ka ewu n'eso*". This literally translates to "the goat follows whoever that is carrying the palm fronds (leaves)"; in Yoruba: enitogbe ewe igiope l'ewure ntele). When we are not goats, why have we lost the intellect to question the character, antecedents, integrity, vision, and experience of the person carrying the palm fronds? Does the source of the *igu* matter? What if it becomes our "last supper" because it is poisoned *igu*? Surprisingly (or not so surprisingly), the elite and the educated doublespeak on this matter: they end up as uncritical followers of people who have nothing to offer. For as long as we downgrade ideas, experience, and exposure and give prominence to *igu* (money) in our political recruitment process, so long shall many countries in Africa, including Nigeria, remain poor".

Who was Pa Jakande before he became a governor and gained prominence in the housing sector? From the Daily Service to the Tribune Newspapers, he was a fearless and intelligent journalist whose editorial contributions were sharp and incisive. He grew up and was moulded in the finest of journalistic traditions. It is in journalism that one marches with the downtrodden, takes risks for others, rebukes abuse of authority, and yet keeps company with the authority with compelling equanimity. A true journalist would, therefore, bring humility to leadership and not be effaced by the trappings of the office, always in tune with his conscience in pursuit of truth and the greater good. Therefore, it is no surprising that most of our notable leaders were journalist: Dr. Nnamdi Azikiwe, Chief Obafemi Awolowo, Chief Anthony Ehahoro, Bisi Onabanjo, Olusegun Osoba, and Adamu Ciroma. This was the company Pa Lateef Jakande kept, and Pa Awolowo helped to nurture and polish his leadership skills. And there could have been no better school for ethical leadership.

Let's remind ourselves that integrity has both economic and moral values. It creates "relationship that produces shared benefits…and creates wealth by making the economy more efficient." In a cute little but important book, The Economics of Integrity[37], Anna Bernasek writes about how integrity "is the invisible infrastructure of the entire economy. It supports everything, holds it together, and allows the economy to work. It's a shared asset that makes us wealthy. Each new relationship based on integrity and trust strengthens and grows the economy. Any relationship that breaks down has a ripple effect throughout the system. That means that every individual has the power to make the economy stronger or weaker. Your integrity matters. Not just to you but to all of us … the true power of integrity comes not from merely appreciating that it exists, but from knowing how to create more." Integrity also means saying that you would do something and doing it. That is what it means to make your word your bond. It means that we should put a new twist on how we deal with corruption. We tend to think that the only anti-corruption message that is effective is: don't steal because we will catch you and punish you. From the statements above, the most effective message is that corruption, the absence of integrity, makes everyone poorer because it reduces the infrastructure for growing the economy. And there is more to corruption and a lack of integrity than financial crimes. When managers and their boards do not show fidelity to the objectives of their organisation but rather use the institution to pursue other objectives, they are subverting the nation and should be categorised as a serious corrupt act. You cannot state one thing in your election manifesto and then completely disregard those promises while claiming integrity. There is no such thing as partial integrity; you either have it or you don't. Integrity is the hallmark of progressive politics because it is fundamentally about trust, a critical element of leadership.

Pa Jakande was schooled in the politics by integrity of Chief Awolowo. I was reading a book on Pa Awolowo titled, *AWO- the Unfinished Greatness: The Life and Times of Obafemi Awolowo*, by Olufemi Ogunsanwo. It gave me an inkling of the school that produced Pa Jakande in terms of having fidelity to the object of government and the integrity and knowledge that he brought to bear in solving the housing problem in Lagos. The free education programmes of Western Nigeria under Pa Awolowo illustrates a leader's fidelity to the object of government and how integrity is the essential competence that allows a vision to come to fruition. Only 35 per cent of children of school age attended school in 1952 in Western Nigeria. Although well researched and articulated, the Pa Awo programmes of universal primary education did not fully anticipate the enthusiasm it would generate or the budgetary implications of this great scheme. This drew skepticism from both British officials and top civil servants. There was a huge gap between the initial estimates that Pa Awo and his team had come up with (about 13 million pounds) for both his universal education and health programme against the total revenue of 5 million pounds. The budget deficit of 8 million pounds was staggering. He cancelled housing subsidies for all civil servants, expatriates, and Nigerians. Rather than cement, they used mud to construct the new schools, and that brought down the cost by about 70 percent. But the capital costs were different from the huge recurrent costs that the programme required. Many were still skeptical and did not know how such a programme could be pulled off. Initial estimates were that in the first year, 175,000 children would enroll in primary school. This estimate was way off target. In January, 1955, when the programme took off, 400,000 children showed up for enrollment. According to Ogunsanwo, "this shook the scheme's logistics to their very foundation". Retired teachers were encouraged to return to the classroom, and new grade 3 teacher-training colleges were established all over the Western Region the next year, producing 11, 000 teachers between 1955-1959. Pa Awolowo's promise to the electorate was that no child would walk more than three kilometres to school, and he kept to the promise, energising communities all over the region. He said, "In achieving the aims of education, the recipient should not unduly suffer by having to attend school too far from home… therefore, schools should be sited in locations that would be easily and almost equally accessible to all children." This was the party manifesto's promise. Despite the difficulties, Pa Awo remained faithful to the object of government and applied knowledge to solve this problem. That is integrity, and this was the school that produced Pa Lateef Jakande. This underscores the critical importance of a leadership recruitment process that is devoid of mercantilism and transaction-driven, but people-focused. Our current politics lack integrity—the manifesto is designed to win elections and has nothing to do with post-election governance. What do the words "progressive" and "people" in the names of our political party mean when our politics is neither progressive nor people-centered. The integrity deficit in this country is staring us all in the face.

Let me end this chapter with a suggestion and an appeal. My suggestion is for the Lagos State government. We want the current Lagos State government to reignite responsible citizenship among Lagosians by passing a law that shows it cares and is willing to create a mindful society. The Social Housing Act should aim to raise funds for low-income public housing through a percentage (10-20%) of tenement rates in Ikoyi, Victoria Island, Lekki, and Ikeja, as well as a percentage of revenues from any land allocation in these areas. The second source of revenue for this fund should be a certain percentage of all accruable taxes and commissions to the state from betting and gambling. [Societies that have allowed betting and gambling have specifically directed the state revenue accruing from this source to social causes—public schooling, etc.] This law should be named the Jakande Act to honour the man who best represents the cause of public housing in Nigeria. I know that I have not put this as elegantly as it should read, but the lawyers, the members of the state assembly, the governor, and the real estate experts can craft this idea into an innovative and model law for the future.

My appeal is to the political and economic elite. When we speak about providing for others or we speak about providing social or public housing, we don't recognise that we are speaking about our community. We are actually speaking about giving a stake to our brothers, sisters, cousins, hairdressers and barbers, our drivers and gardeners, and our cooks and watchmen. We are really speaking about helping ourselves. We are one community. So, as we leave here today, let us advocate for low-income public housing because it is good for us. Just remember that the strength of this nation or any nation lies in our pulling everyone up. It is not a sign of weakness to help the weak.

PART THREE
National Development Planninig and Shared Prosperity

CHAPTER SIX

Development Planning For Inclusiveness in an Uncommon Environment

Development is the resolution of our many contradictions

1
The Context of Development and Planning

Development planning presupposes that there is an unambiguous agreement on what development means and that this definitional consensus, whatever the elements are, can be planned. The means for attaining development are even more contentious. On all scores, there are different schools of thought. It is this lack of agreement that has led to those who insist that: sustained economic growth would lead to development and that the state should stay out of the way except in the provision of the so-called *enabling environment*; others contend that economic growth is not enough and that we need inclusive growth; others insist that the capitalist market system is wired inherently to produce uneven growth and wide income inequality and therefore that we need inclusive development; and yet others insist that it can only be called development if it is fair. Both inclusive and fair development proponents assign a strong role to a developmental state. And I have argued that the efficacy of the developmental state is underpinned by leaders with the right attitude and citizens who have imbibed the right values. Many have also argued that a holistic approach to development must, in addition to the material dimension, also recognise the spiritual, cultural, and ethical dimensions of development, and therefore warn Africans not to pursue economic development that lacks a moral and cultural content. As the late distinguished political economist, Prof. Claude Ake, eloquently argued in his seminal book, *Democracy and Development in Africa*, "development is an ideology" an ideology that sometimes sees your culture as an impediment to your development[38]. In a paper I delivered in 2008 on "Intellectuals and Development", I argued that in the pursuit of truth, not clearly defined, intellectuals may be pursuing a development agenda as presented by other people's values, wearing the cloak of objectivity and inevitability but lacking in material relevance to our context.[39] [If you take the one dollar a day measure of poverty and evaluate it within our context, where most of our assets, especially rural assets and services, have non-market value, it can become quite problematic. But let's not get distracted here.]

For Amartya Sen, development is the "process of expanding the real freedoms that people enjoy." In his best-selling book, *Development as Freedom*, the Nobel Prize-winning economist, argued that narrowly focusing on economic growth, rising personal incomes, industrialisation or technological advances, or social modernisation misses the point. According to him, these are means to an end. Viewing development in terms of substantial improvement in freedoms, he suggests that it "requires the removal of major sources of unfreedom: poverty as well as tyranny, poor economic opportunities as well as systematic social deprivation, neglect of public facilities, and intolerance or overactivity of repressive states." [40]

2
Development as Resolution of Contradictions

I find Professor Sen's argument very appealing given our history and current socio-economic context and its many contradictions. For me, development is the resolution of our many contradictions: we have had both the military dictatorship and civilian governments, and a seemingly buoyant but acquiescing civil society; we have many rules and laws but they are observed in breach; we have presence of schools but absence of learning[41]; we have huge banking industry profits, but very little credit to the real sector; we have huge and rising debts, but very dilapidated and neglected public social and economic infrastructure; we have increasing growth rate without declining poverty; We consume what is manufactured elsewhere, but our manufacturing sector is insignificant; we have many jobbers but rising joblessness and underemployment (that lead to irresponsible citizenship, mutual distrust and loss of dignity); large number of micro-producers and traders but very few micro-entrepreneurs; many people are working but only very few are making a living; we are good consumers of technology but poor producers of technology; a growing quantitative youth bulging with a corresponding quality-capability decline (the need to focus on our population explosion); high female population with poor gender equity; we have a voiceless majority that have minority social and political power; we are a federation but unitary in practice; we have extremely rich people living side by side with extremely poor people; we have a moral quagmire of religious ascendancy but value decadence. That these contradictions exist in the first place is symptomatic of the absence of an ideology – an attitude (values and knowledge) espoused by a leadership that has its eyes fixed on creating shared prosperity and a caring society.

Therefore, it doesn't really matter your persuasion. We can therefore accept that development, in our context, requires the resolution of the many prevalent socio-economic contradictions as a means of improving the overall wellbeing of the generality of the citizens of Nigeria in a manner that guarantees their liberty of choice as active participants in the economic, social, political, and cultural spaces. Can these be resolved by market forces and private-sector-led growth alone, or can the state work with the private sector through a planning exercise to influence the quality of growth and the sources of growth? In other words, how central is planning to tackling the sources of these contradictions? If development is ultimately the "civilization of being" and not of having, because of the limit of expansion of output, in the words of Louis-Joseph Lebret, it also necessitates an "equitable sharing of having" [42] and what I have elsewhere called the civilization of love and pursuit of happiness. [43]This is more so with the discordant global market economy, where the global financial crisis and the consequent bailouts exposed the underbelly of the often touted pillars of the market economy-discipline, efficiency, and "creative destruction".

3
Planning In an Uncommon Environment

So, what is national planning? National planning is a process of articulating and coordinating a strategic set of activities, projects, and programmes that translate a collective national vision into an improvement in the overall well-being of her citizens. These activities, projects and programmes must address the many contradictions of our time. But there is a problem. National planning assumes a collective national vision, a sense of nation, a common identity, and a common aspiration. We shall return to this later. Planning is an interactive process involving dialogue, negotiations, trade-offs, contractual obligations, benchmarking, evaluation, feedback, concrete outcomes, and mechanisms for anticipating and dealing with intended and unintended effects. It is strategic because during the plan period, priorities must be identified in a coherent and coordinated manner, with the aim of achieving a few carefully selected goals. In an International Labor Organization Working Paper, *Inclusive Development Strategy in an Era of Globalization,* Ignacy Sachs sums up the process as follows: "planning is an iterative process including both bottom-up and top-down procedures, requiring the framework of a long-term national project, a vision shared by the majority of the nation's citizens concerning values, and translation into societal goals." [44]These goals can be short, medium, or long-term.

It is important to note that a national development plan based on shared vision rests on discipline, committed leadership, a strong sense of duty, a heavy dose of patriotism, and transformational bureaucracy. It is the strong sense of a respect for rules and conformity, what Adam Smith calls "propriety," the prioritisation of honest and upright behavior, and respect for values that would prevent corruption. One of the many ways in which to gauge the direction and outcomes of social change among different nations is to observe their sense of duty—their ruled-based behaviour. It is difficult to have effective national development plans in a corruption-infested environment. Corruption blurs the sense of national vision, reducing goals to primordial objectives often driven by personal, regional, or ethnic gains. When budgets are inflated unduly in the National Assembly in Nigeria, as we have seen in the past, it is an act of corruption. It does not matter whether they are induced to do so by corrupt heads of Ministries Departments and Agencies (MDAs). In a national planning framework, this is likely to distort the alignment of the budget with stated goals, be they short-, medium- or long-term. But is it possible that the National Assembly acts out of what it may term a sense of "relative justice", merely acting in accordance with the "prevailing behavioural norm", and because the actors in the executive are doing it and getting away with it?

But to use the word "justice" to justify corruption is to deodorise a reproachable act. It is clear from this discussion that the current administration's emphasis on eradicating corruption, as difficult as this may seem, is strategic and well-placed. Without arresting it, no development plan can have meaning, for development plans have an inbuilt sense of shared sacrifice, trust, compromise, ethics, and equity, including inter-generational equity. And it is important that the fight be led exemplarily from the top because there is some evidence that corruption is imitative, and corruption at the top leadership level has serious indirect consequences. We quote Chinese author Hui-nan Tzu in 122 B.C. from Amartya Sen's book:

> If the measuring line is true, then the wood will be straight, not because one makes a special effort but because that which it is "ruled" by makes it so. In the same way, if the ruler is sincere and upright, then honest officials will serve in his government and scoundrels will go into hiding, but if the ruler is not upright, then evil men will have their way and loyal men will retire to seclusion.[45]

These are wise words. But in addition to leading by example, what else should the ruler or leader do? It is important to block leakages, but the emphasis must be on changing the norms of behaviour among senior civil servants, the political leadership, and any person in a position of power and authority. To change behaviour and force compliance with rules, it involves incentives and punishments as well as institutional reforms. The thief has to be punished, but those responsible for catching the thief and charged with implementing the rules must be incentivized to avoid capture. The allure to privatise public resources should not be sentimentalised. In our environment, this allure is made worse by the general attitude of the populace towards corruption, which encourages people in authority to grab their share and bring it home. We have to realise that we are no longer dealing with corruption as an aberrant behaviour but with a culture of corruption, with most people wanting *to chop* from where they work or, in many instances, where they do not even work. We must, therefore, make citizens active and disciplined participants in the change process. They must realise that if we are going to plan for our collective future, they cannot be seen to be condemning and condoning corruption at the same time, booing when it concerns someone else but cheering when the culprit is one of their own or waiting in the wings to join in the gravy train. It is not an easy task for Aristotle, who reminds us thus:

> I count him braver who overcomes his desires than him who conquers his enemies; for the hardest victory is over self.

And Theodore Roosevelt, the 26th President of the United States, added: "With self-discipline, almost anything is possible." If we must plan effectively for the future and resolve the socio-economic contradictions that currently exist, we must not only have a disciplined environment; we must have disciplined citizens imbued with broader values, nationalistic concerns, sacrifice, and ethics.

4
Salient Issues with Nigeria's Experience with Development Planning

Nigeria has had a checkered history of development planning. There were four of them before 1999, the beginning of the new democratic dispensation. These plans were: 1962-68; 1970-75; 1976-80; and 1981-85. These plans were: 1962–68; 1970–75; 1976–80; and 1981–85. Following 1999, we had the 2004 National Economic Empowerment and Development Strategy [NEEDS] and the Obasanjo-inspired and Yar'Adua-adopted Vision 20: 2020. It is not my intention to review these plans here. For a detailed review, see Ajakaiye (2014, 2015)[46]; Obadan (1994, 1996); Ikeanyibe (2009)[47] and several other scholars. But I want to make a few points:

1. That apart from the first two plans, which built on one another, others were almost stand alone; ideologically both recognised Nigeria as a mixed economy, but the second plan of 1970-75 was more forcefully mixed by injecting government more directly into economic activities. The lessons from the first plan, in addition to the oil revenue, may have influenced this trajectory;
2. That planning in a non-democratic environment is problematic, if not defective *ab initio*. Effective planning is consultative and participatory, top-down and bottom-up, requiring strong and

credible institutions. Military regimes are notorious for lacking these sensibilities.

3. But where democratic structures are weak, there must be an elite consensus. More than anything else, elite consensus on politics, economy, and culture is critical for shaping the future developmental trajectory of any nation. [The discordant tune we experience between the executive and legislature in Nigeria is exemplary of elite discord; in spite of the so-called *espirit de corps*, the military lacked it, as was illustrated by the number of coups Nigeria had];

4. Planning in a federal system requires strong leadership and strong institutions at the various tiers of government. Planning agencies are among the least funded. The Joint Planning Board that brings the National Planning Commission and the State Planning Agencies together did not meet for several years. When they met, it did not often carry the commitment of the leadership and citizenry they represent, and the joint resolutions were often not implemented;

5. The NEEDS document was a cleverly crafted plan. However, it was born in an environment of peer envy, the absence of a hands-on guardian, a lack of agreement on the role of planning in a regime that was decidedly pro-market in her reform, bad politics, and poor governance at the state and local levels;

6. The decoupling of budget, especially capital budget, from planning is a fundamental problem. It did not allow for budgetary discipline and commitment. The envelope system of budgeting was too *laissez faire*; it was not strictly priority-driven and was not tied to a long-term plan or vision. The medium-term expenditure framework was ad hoc and lacked depth. Budget allocation was driven by the standing of a minister in the eyes of the allocating ministry. The budgeting process was further complicated by the National Assembly.

7. The Vision 20: 2020 document was inspired by an external assessment, adopted by President Obasanjo in 2006, and subsequently finalised by President Yar'Adua in 2009. The Vision 20: 2020 was a long-term plan intended to give birth to medium-term plans that would be implemented through annual budgets. In my view, it was a very well-thought-out plan with goals, targets, milestones, and an implementation strategy. It suffered from the death of President Yar'Adua and the institutional arrangement that decoupled the budget from planning.

Subsequently, it became a slogan, but no reference was made to it in any of the subsequent budget documents or presentations.

5
The Imperative of Leadership, Shared Vision, and Sense of Nation

- Lessons from Other Nations –

- Underlying many of these difficulties with planning is the absence of shared vision and a sense of nation among the ruling elite. Shared vision allows for credible commitment, which ties the hands of the leaders and allows institutions to deliver on their mandate. Credible commitment requires discipline, sacrifice, the right attitude, and consistency of purpose. Why is the vision of the executive different from that of the legislature? How can you set up a Petroleum Technology Development Fund (PTDF) and allow it to do things other than developing technology for Nigerians to have some control of the oil industry? Why would a regime change abort a national vision or change the mandate of a strategic national institution? How can you plan under undisciplined leadership without a clear national sense of purpose?

A sense of nation means that a South Eastern leader must see reason and advocate for allocating national resources to the development of the North East because it is in the national interest to do so. Just the same way, a policy to support an automotive industry in the east must receive the support of all rather than be encumbered because policymakers are inefficiently searching for other geopolitical equivalents in order to balance the support to the detriment of the nation. There are affirmative actions that affirm and build a sense of nation, but there are others that destroy it. In development planning, we must recognise our sectoral and regional strengths and build on them in order to deal with our weaknesses, realising that they are our common strengths and weaknesses. In Nigeria, the prism of assessment or consideration is, for the most part, not Nigeria, not common purpose; our imagination is tied to other parochial considerations.

In his book, From Third World to First, the father of modern Singapore, the late Lee Kuan Yew, stated unequivocally in the early days of their independence that they were building an inclusive society where every Singaporean would share in its development as well as in its prosperity. And that is what he has built: a fair nation, a Singapore, where everyone has a stake in its prosperity, and he did that using what he called an *"honest and effective government that people must elect"*. He did it by planning with a common purpose, a shared vision, and a sense of nation. Lee Kuan Yew achieved the inclusive transformation of Singapore through disciplined leadership, disciplined citizenship, and by disciplining the environment. He did it by sheer hard work, by being detail-oriented, and in his words, "by setting out to recruit the best into government", by not leaving leadership to chance or allowing the politics of Singapore to be dominated by what he called "political activists". [48] We must ask ourselves, what is the leadership recruitment process in this country? How can you plan in an environment dominated by those who do not see tomorrow?

In 2012, President Barack Obama acknowledged that the technologies that enabled the private sector to extract natural gas from shale oil came from the investment of the federal government in research over 30 years. Here, President Obama was acknowledging that the United States is a developmental state: its federal government uses public resources, in a smart way—support for research—to support and subsidise private initiative in pursuit of industrial policy by other means. He revealed the consistency of the federal government in pursuing a strategic goal, irrespective of the party in power. He further revealed the credible commitment that allows institutions to rise above politics and stay on course with their mandate. Obama's statement demonstrated that even though there is no national planning agency, there is a plan, a multi-year plan to help actualise a vision. In this case, the planning for the development of a technology that cracked open the shale rock for oil and gas took 30 years of investment. It is the same determination and planning that led to the translation of President Kennedy's vision in 1962 that Americans would land someone on the moon into reality in 1969.

It is important to note that in 1982, when the Federal government started the investment Obama referred to, he was 21 years old and an undergraduate. Since 1982, you've had three Republican presidents and two Democratic presidents. But the investment in the search for this technology was uninterrupted. It is equally worthy of note that while the Federal government was investing, it was clear that some states where the shale rock deposit exists would benefit more than the others, but that did not deter the various governments from funding the research. No one argued against this investment because the territory that would benefit most did not vote for the party in power. [49]

In 1982, when Dr. Mahathir Mohamad was running for the election that would make him the Prime Minister of Malaysia, he chose the slogan: clean, efficient, and trustworthy. In his memoir, A Doctor in the House, he said that he knew that Malays disliked change. But he knew that Malaysia would not develop if they stuck to their old ways. According to him, "I always believed that things could be done differently and that value systems determine the success or otherwise of an individual, a community, or a nation. While the values of a community or nation develop naturally, they can also be deliberately inculcated, and the best way to do this is for the government to practise these values." He set up a plan to clean up corruption, promote efficiency and trustworthiness. In explaining why nations fail, distinguished economists Acemoglu and Robinson noted that "the extent to which people trust each other and cooperate is important" as a products of their institutions and politics. What was the result of Malaysia's campaign to clean-up corruption? According to the Prime Minister, the Customs Department was efficient in collecting monies due to the government; in his words, "the government has always had enough money to pay salaries and the cost of development projects without borrowing. We were also always able to tide over financial crises that came our way because we were financially strong. Most other countries would not have been able to do what we did."

In order to create a sense of shared vision and fair distribution of prosperity in Malaysia, a new economic policy was formulated in 1971. Essentially, the government realised that if the majority Malay were excluded from the mainstream economy, as was the case prior to the implementation of the new economic policy, the country would not make much progress. Malaysia is a multi-ethnic country with a majority of Malays and a minority of Chinese and Indians. In resolving, in part, what Dr. Mahatir Mohamad called the "Malay Dilemma", the New Economic Policy sought to give every ethnic group a sense of belonging and a stake in their country, then and in the prosperity of her future. This economic affirmative action created the peace and elite consensus required to plan for the orderly development of their country on their own terms. Today, Malays operate in every strata of the Malaysian economy as mechanics, business owners, and chief executives of companies through a deliberate policy that suits their circumstances. But this was still a work in progress.

In 1991, the idea of a long-term plan occurred to the leadership of Malaysia, and they turned to the Institute of Strategic and International Studies (ISIS) to develop a conceptual blueprint that articulated their social, economic, and political paths—a 30-year plan dubbed Vision 2020—which outlined what Malaysia needed to do to be a developed country. The target was a USD 16, 000 per capita income and an average growth rate of seven percent for the 30-year period.

In the consultation and launch that followed this vision 2020, the Prime Minister indicated that he would, in his words, "first establish a single, united Malaysian nation." He said, "Though born of different races, all Malaysians had to see themselves as nationals of one and the same country. Different though we were in our origins, ours was a common destiny. We might also differ politically, but our loyalty and dedication to the nation had to be unshakeable. We were all, without reservation or limitation, part of *Bangsa Malaysia* —a single Malaysian people, unified yet diverse —a Malaysia where you are free to express your historical identity but not in a separatist form." And he said something else that is very important. He wanted "Malaysia to develop and be modern according to our own historic pattern with our own distinct ethical and moral values intact—not by aping others and losing our soul."[50]

The Vision 2020 provided a platform for planning, intelligent risk-taking, investing in research, innovation and changing the mindset of immediate return by realising that the product of research takes a long time to materialise. Malaysia launched its 11th five-year plan (2016-2020) in 2015, with the goal of becoming a developed country by 2020. Her current per capita income is USD 11, 371 and that of Nigeria is USD 2, 085, with a life expectancy of 76.51 years as opposed to 55.44 years in Nigeria. This is a country that Nigeria was way ahead of at independence. Today, Nigeria is sending our engineering students on scholarship to Malaysian universities.

We turn to China to illustrate a sense of shared vision and how to build on regional advantages driven by a new leadership ideology crafted on their own terms. China has three city groups as economic growth poles: the Yangtze River Delta, which is centred on Shanghai, the Pearl River Delta, which is centred on Guangzhou and Shenzhen, and the Jing-jin-yi, which is centred on Tianjin, with a fourth planned. According to Chinese scholars, Lin Ling and Liu Shi-Quin of the Sichuan Academy of Sciences, the development strategy of China gave priority to the development of the eastern region first, where these three growth poles exist. That planning started in the East was predicated on the unique territorial advantages of the East. But these Eastern growth poles, according to these academics, have made great contributions to the economic and social development of China. They contributed more than 41 percent of all economic aggregates in China. The fourth pole was planned in the West, the Chengdu-Chongqing Zone, aimed at forming a network with the three earlier zones in the East and intended to achieve a balanced and coordinated regional development around the country.[51] In the 12th national development plan of China (2011-2015), the development of Western China was clearly stated as a goal. In addition to the other goals of developing seven priority industries, inclusive growth, increasing domestic consumption, improving energy efficiency, moving into high-end manufacturing, improving the lives of ordinary Chinese, and reduction in income inequality.[52] The lessons are clear: an effective development plan must build on the territorial advantages of each region. You cannot create these advantages where they do not initially exist. However, in order to achieve a more balanced, inclusive, and coordinated development, the return on investment in the advantaged region can be used to plan and create other economic growth poles. This kind of planning requires strong leadership, a broad mindset, a sense of shared vision, and a commitment to long-term planning.

Today, China is on the verge of her 13th development plan (2016-2020). And the world waited with great expectation as the Chinese Communist Party held its fifth plenum to discuss the five year plan that is designed to enable her break into advanced country status with a projected per capita income of over USD 13,000 by 2020-2024. The reason why the world is interested in the Chinese plan is that there is an elite consensus around it, and from experience, the plan has in-built credibility and would guide the policy direction of China for the next five years.

6
Nigeria: A Proposed Course of Action

It is clear that, given the contradictions identified earlier, we need to plan. The failure of the market further exposed by the global financial crisis, has given development planning additional impetus for a country like Nigeria. In Eboh and Ogbu (2010), I stated that "the market is good, but the new realities have forced the need to deepen the governance of the market. This would require new institutions, the widening of the tax base, and robust regulatory systems that are transparent, credible, and effective." I called for a renewed attention to development planning in what I called the "new market economy".[53] We need planning, let's then look at the institutional mechanisms for our planning.

Institutional Mechanism: The National Planning Commission (NPC)

The agency of government responsible for national planning in Nigeria is the National Planning Commission under the presidency. It is important that this is under the Presidency and that it is national and not a federal planning agency. Its status as a national planning agency reflects part of its mandate as the coordinating institution between the federal, state, and local governments as well as the secretariat of the National Economic Council. In Malaysia, they have the Economic Planning Unit under the Prime Minister's office responsible for implementing the decisions of the National Planning Council, which is the economic arm of the cabinet, similar to our economic team, even though our economic team is not institutionalised.

I would propose that we retain the National Planning Commission but strengthen it as follows:

a. To make it truly national by bringing into the national planning process, six regional planning CEOs representing the six geopolitical zones. This means that the six zones should create six planning agencies that can deal with their local planning and implementation while cascading certain issues to the national planning commission. There is a semblance of this emerging already, but it needs inspiration from the top. The six members plus the Minister of National Planning shall form the National Planning Consultative Committee. This committee shall have the responsibility of liaising with the private sector, NGOs, and the legislature. The report of this committee is presented to the National Economic Council and ultimately to the President; (details of this can be worked out). This process is useful in building on regional strengths and in planning and executing projects that ensure fairness and inclusivity. I am tempted to suggest that since national integration (shared vision) is so important in a planning process, this becomes part of the mandate of the new National Planning Commission;

b. The National Planning Commission should be transformed into the Think Tank of government, funded, staffed, and remunerated appropriately with a new mentality, work ethics, orientation, and efficiency. [I started this process in 2006, but the gains were quickly reversed when I left the Commission]. India, led by Prime Minister Narendra Modi during its 12th five year plan (2012-2016), abolished the Planning Commission and replaced it with the National Institute for Transforming India and introduced members from the regional governments into the Institute[54] –I guessed this is to signal that it is not planning as usual.

Integrate the Budget Office with the National Planning Commission

The budget office should move from the Ministry of Finance to the National Planning Commission (NPC) for the following reasons:

- development planning is less effective and impactful without simultaneous control and diligent monitoring of the capital budget by one institution — the planning institution.
- it is the budget that drives the plan, and the integration of both in one institution is best practice in many emerging countries.
- the current practise of the Ministry of Finance in preparing the Medium-Term Expenditure Framework (MTEF) to go with the budget is sub-optimal.

- MTEF is a short-term plan when Nigeria actually needs an annual budget, medium-term plans, and long-term plans;
- Long-term planning makes for budget discipline and policy continuity;
- Long-term planning forces MDAs to stay with identified priorities and constrains the National Assembly from imposing its will on the budget;
- To avert the limitation on long-term planning imposed by the four-year electoral cycle, Nigeria should think of promulgating her long-term plans into laws as an act of the National Assembly—it might change the nature of the plan to allow for differences in details from one regime to another without altering the main trusts, targets, and outcomes.
- Finance does not have the skills for planning and approaches this process in an ad-hoc manner.
- If budget was driven by a plan, it would expose the oversimplification of the current envelope system, where budget amounts are allocated to MDAs and they internally decide how to allocate **them**— this process is fraught with lazy thinking, with budget amounts allocated without being in tandem with agreed national development priorities. How can one explain the tripling of the budget of a ministry in one year —did the national priority suddenly change?
- MDAs brag about the size of their budget envelopes rather than the services provided with the funds. No one is monitoring.
- In a dwindling revenue environment, with a compelling need to diversify the economy, create gainful employment, and engineer inclusive growth, we do not have a choice but to define the priorities tightly (i.e., plan) and budget accordingly to drive the plan. The plan must therefore roll from year to year. This has worked extremely well for Malaysia and other emerging economies. This is how to avoid the so-called "abandoned project syndrome".

Sectoral and Technological Plan

- In national development planning, there are key institutions that must work in concert towards a critical sectoral goal(s) or towards achieving a certain technological milestone; technological planning is a long-term endeavour requiring consistency of funding, risk-taking and serious coordination between the public and private sectors. Coordination is required between the development banks, key science and technology institutions, the universities, and the private sector. The president's authority is required for this coordination to be effective, and this authority can be exercised by proxy through the NPC.

- Moving the budget office to the National Planning Commission will create room for the Ministry of Finance to focus on its treasury function.

7
Budgeting For Inclusiveness

In addition to our medium and long-term plans and the associated budget outlays targeting the resolution of the identified socio-economic contradictions, especially income and regional inequalities, as a means of fostering inclusiveness, there is one additional proposal. Another way in which we can engineer our budget for poverty reduction and inclusiveness is to set aside a certain proportion of our annual budget for the poorest segment of society. We can set aside about 3 to 4 per cent of the annual budget and allocate it according to the poverty profile of each federal constituency—the poorer the constituency, the higher the allocation. The National Bureau of Statistics has the poverty map of the country, and this is not expected to generate much controversy. But for this to work, there must be a sense of shared vision, a sense of one nation. Second, a local implementation committee, which must have men and women of integrity with community consciousness, is a critical requirement. They would be charged with identifying local projects and programmes that improve the assets and productivity of the poor and working towards addressing them with the allocated budget. This is one process that can challenge and test the quality of the governance and politics at the state and local governments and showcase our willingness to have a fair society.

Development planning is still required in Nigeria in order to address the many contradictions that exist in our socio-economic environment. No one doubts the useful role of the market in allocating resources, but the market needs to be governed in profound and creative ways. The global financial crisis has given additional impetus for government intervention in the conduct of economic activities beyond regulation and the provision of an enabling environment.

Long-, medium-, and short- term planning are required to provide the framework under which the private sector would operate, deal with intended and unintended effects of the market economy, and ensure inclusive participation by all segments of society.

Experience and history have taught us that both industrial and technological advancement, hence development, do not occur naturally. They require systematic planning and the implementation of intelligent, directed, and coordinated policies that an honest government with a strong leadership must implement. Strong institutions and credible commitments that tie the hands of political actors are very important. Bad politics leading to disjointed policies, corruption, budget indiscipline, poor execution capacity, and partial solutions would undermine national development planning.

We recommend the strengthening of the National Planning Commission in order to improve its intellectual leadership, effectiveness, and efficiency. In particular, we suggest the injection of zonal planning coordinators into the process in order to improve the bottom-up consultations, legitimise the process, and improve ownership and implementation at the zonal and state levels. We also recommend that the budget office be moved to the National Planning Commission in order to give teeth to the planning process, ensure consistency of the budget, and discipline and accountability of actors. For greater accountability, the civil society must be empowered to monitor and evaluate implementation of the plan and issue reports on a regular basis. Inclusiveness in development planning would require allocating a certain percentage of the budget on the basis of the poverty ranking of the federal constituencies.

Experiences from elsewhere suggest that planning cannot produce the desired result in a corrupt environment. Greed and short-term gains cannot align with long-term planning. Both the environment and the citizens must be disciplined. But above all, leadership must create a sense of shared vision and a sense of nation before development planning can create a fair society.

CHAPTER SEVEN

In Search Of Inclusive Growth: Reducing Unemployment and Poverty in Africa's Growing Economies

I suggest that Africa's growth, if not driven by a diversified production structure, essentially by growth in manufacturing that would deliver lots of quality jobs, raise productivity and incomes, it would remain trepid, fragile, and susceptible to negative shocks.

1

There is currently a celebratory tone about Africa's recent growth and continued prospects. This is as a result of very impressive economic growth of over 6% in many African countries in the past several years. Unfortunately, unemployment and poverty persist. We briefly interrogate the sources of Africa's growth and explain the continued dominance of primary production, export, and low-value addition. I suggest that Africa's growth, if not driven by a diversified production structure, essentially by growth in manufacturing that would deliver lots of quality jobs, raise productivity and incomes, would remain trepid, fragile, and susceptible to negative shocks. Poverty is likely to persist without a robust formal manufacturing sector where innovation and technology would improve value addition and raise productivity. And there is an emerging consensus on a new industrial and technology policy regime that, if well-crafted, contextualised and implemented, could stimulate greater manufacturing in Africa and lead to permanent structural change.

2
Africa's Fragile Growth and Its Discontent

In its December 2011 edition, the Economist ran a cover story, [55]"Africa rising", detailing Africa's growth performance. It was reported that "at least a dozen African countries have expanded by more than 6 percent a year for six or more years". Inflation is down, average per capita income is also rising, telephone penetration is increasing, and there is relative political stability, according to the report. This is all good news. The Economist concludes that "Africa's growth is underpinned by a permanent shift in expectations" and quotes an African Development Bank executive who characterised the "boom" as representing a "structural change." As an African scholar and an economist, I was intrigued because there is danger in the untold half of the story.

The arguments for a growth-centered model for lifting millions in developing countries out of poverty appear unassailable until we are confronted with the case of most African countries, including Nigeria.

Prof. Jagdish Bhagwati, a distinguished international economist, recently argued that growing the economy was the sure way, if not the only way, to lift people out of poverty. According to Bhagwati, "growth would pull the poor into gainful employment, thereby helping to lift them out of poverty…and that higher incomes would enable them to increase their personal spending on education and health."[56] Yet, economic growth in Nigeria has not created meaningful employment, as many of the country's youth, including those with university degrees, are currently unemployed or underemployed. In addition, the incomes of the majority of Nigerians have not risen, and while access to education and health may have improved in the country, their quality has declined significantly.

Africa's growth is still very fragile. In spite of the impressive growth rates, Africa's economic transformation has not occurred, and any talk of a structural shift is not backed by evidence. No doubt, Africa's growth is driven by rising commodity prices. Agriculture with low productivity dominates the economies, with yields far below international standards. Increases in output result from extensification, which involves bringing more land under cultivation (with serious environmental consequences), rather than intensification, which would necessitate the use of appropriate technologies. Sub-Sahara Africa fertilizer consumes 17kg of fertiliser per hectare, compared to 159kg in South Asia and 135kg globally. Exports are still dominated by primary commodities and minerals. Primary commodity exports account for 90 per cent of all exports from sub-Saharan Africa (excluding South Africa), and Africa's share of global manufacturing export is 0.5 per cent.

To underscore that a structural shift has not occurred, it is important to examine the manufacturing sector's contribution to GDP in the growing African countries: Nigeria (7% after rebasing); Kenya (11.5); Ghana (8.5); Botswana (3.6); Tanzania (6.9); Senegal (13.9); Ethiopia (5.3); Rwanda (8.5); Cameroon (18.1); and Mauritius (19.1).[57] Compare that to the significance of the manufacturing sector in emerging economies where structural change is occurring: Brazil (20); China (34); Malaysia (30); Thailand (35); and Indonesia (28). Africa's commodity boom has also turned into an import boom, with Africa importing basic manufacture goods that it should produce. Rather than use the foreign exchange she earns to import technology and acquire the skills necessary for the structural change. Until recently, and thanks to agricultural reform, Nigeria spent about $8 million per day on food imports. That is the other side of the story. Borrowing from President Obama, this is not the character of an "economy build to last."

The same economist that was extolling the growth rates admitted rather awkwardly that "a long-term decline in commodity prices would undoubtedly hurt" but added a sweetener that "Africa's commodities now have a wide range of buyers," mistakenly laying more emphasis on the diversification of demand rather than on the urgent need for diversification and the production and export of sophisticated products that would truly signal a structural change. Africa's growth is now tied, limitedly, to the boom in India and China and their need for commodities and oil. That is not how sustainable growth with jobs is constructed. That is not how development takes place. Development, according to Danny Rodrick, a distinguished economist, is "fundamentally about structural change"[58]. As I read the economist's piece, I could not help but scream deja vu! It appears that the old-age conviction that Africa should continue to do "what she does best"— provide raw materials for the industrialisation of other continents—is still with us. Yet, we are reminded that the driving force for economic development, according to Dani Rodrick, "cannot be the forces of comparative advantage as conventionally understood. The trick seems to be to acquire mastery over a broader range of activities, instead of concentrating on what one does best." [59]

3

The New Opportunity for Industrial Policy in Africa and What Other Nations Did

We are speaking at a time when Africa has new vistas of opportunity to reengineer its industrial base, expand manufacturing, create meaningful jobs, and foster inclusive growth. First, there is the emergence of a policy space as a result of the writings and utterances of political leaders and scholars all over the world who are now embracing the partnership between the state and the market as necessary for re-engineering growth with jobs in what can be described as a forceful support for and return to open industrial policy. Second, the rising commodity and mineral prices provide the foreign exchange and revenue that would be used to source technology, capital goods, and equipment, as well as to offer "smart subsidies" that are market friendly. Third, the seemingly declining Chinese competitiveness in the lower-end manufacturing sector opens up additional opportunity for Africa to exploit.

The return to open industrial policy is echoing in Washington, Davos, and Europe. In Obama's State of the Union address in January 2012, we saw this in his proposal for getting the American economy growing with jobs, in his strong push for "an economy build to last." Reports from the 2012 World Economic Forum in Davos indicate that European leaders such as Angela Merkel of Germany expressed the same sentiments about the need for companies to be patriotic and keep manufacturing jobs at home. Speakers at the September 2010 Liberal Democratic Party annual event urged the UK government to engineer greater collaboration between industry and business, stressing that "the UK needs to stop coming up with great inventions only to leave it to others to exploit them and move from invention towards innovation". [60] Rana Foroohar's report in Time magazine in February 2013, [61]Economist Clyde Prestowitz and the Dean of Harvard Business School, Nitin Nohria, all believe that companies, for good reasons, do have obligations towards the home market. And governments are now ready to help them, whether they stay or return home. What does this assistance from the state entail? Policy actions, pronouncements, and scholarly writings have since tended to suggest that what was earlier termed a "fragile consensus" is solidifying. As Dani Rodrick puts it convincingly, "it is increasingly recognised that developing societies need to embed private initiative in a framework of public action that encourages restructuring, diversification, and technological dynamism beyond what market forces on their own would generate."[62] If there are skeptics, they are those constrained by their deep ideological conviction rather than accepting the reality of hard evidence.

The use of industrial policy to engineer industrialisation is not new. That the industrialised economies of the West are returning to it more forcefully in order to create jobs at home, in a dialogue that mixes patriotism with state support, may be new.

It has always been industrial policy by other means in the West, particularly in the United States, to use public resources to subsidise industrial research, often targeted at a specific industry. In the West, especially in the United States, it has always been, industrial policy by other means. In the United States, public investment in research is frequently directed towards the private sector, with the goal of assisting them in taking risks in new areas or developing new technology. This is confirming that science-led development is a leadership endeavor, requiring strong resource support, tenacity, staying the course, and, above all, belief in the capacity of your scientists.

Others used more explicit policies to support strategic industries. Ha-Joon Chang[63], a Cambridge University economist, chronicles the history of the use of industrial policy by the industrialised West and the emerging economies of China, South Korea and Singapore in his book, Bad Samaritans. He noted that Finland, Norway, Italy and Austria, "were all relatively backward at the end of the Second World War and saw the need for rapid industrial development – used strategies similar to those used by Japan and France to promote their industries." Those strategies include "indicative planning that channeled investment (flow of credit) into strategic industries through state-owned banks; industrial tariffs maintained at a relatively high level until 1960; tight control of imports; local content requirements of foreign investment; targeted subsidies; and export marketing support, etc." According to him, "the strategy worked very well". By the 1980s, he stated, "France had transformed itself into a technology leader in many areas." As for his home country, South Korea, Chang was emphatic that "the Korean Economic Miracle was a result of a clever and pragmatic mixture of market incentives and state direction". In Korea, under the Park administration, the Economic Planning Board (similar to our National Planning Commission) was launched in 1961 and charged with developing five-year plans, annual budget preparation, and coordination of foreign aid and foreign investment. According to a recent report by the Brookings Institution authored by Homi Khras and others, "planning was linked to budget… and foreign aid was linked to both planning and budget. And the Park administration maintained a policy of focusing on large-scale manufacturing enterprises that were import-substitution or export-oriented despite the recommendations of U.S. advisers to focus more on small and medium-sized enterprises." Under Park administration, "instead of penalising corrupt businessmen, Park expropriated their bank stocks and assigned them to invest in key import-substitution industries such as fertilizers."[64] One of the key institutions for economic restructuring was the Korean Institute for Science and Technology, established with the assistance of the United States but with a strong Korean orientation, with the primary aim of institutionalising the learning process and mastering and domesticating technology. There are huge lessons for Nigeria here.

To some extent, the current environment presents both a challenge and an opportunity; the opportunity of technological adaptation as a result of the "tipping point" of Chinese lower-end manufacturing as well as the challenge of putting in place the necessary building blocks for a successful manufacturing sector. India, China, and South Korea present Africa with huge lessons on what works and how to avoid the pitfalls of the past. Interestingly, whether it is in the use of smart subsidies, building domestic skills and technological capability, enforcing domestic content requirements, work ethics, value reorientation, maintaining macroeconomic stability, or the return or use of diaspora, Africa has a lot to learn from China and India. So how do we move from made in China to made in Kenya, Nigeria, Senegal, Ghana or Tanzania?

The Focus on Manufacturing

Manufacturing is critical for sustained inclusive growth, innovation, and the creation of quality jobs. Hence, Africa's structural shift will come from rapid growth in the manufacturing sector.

Africa also needs growth that can address the growing inequality in African economies that leads to youth restiveness and insecurity. The manufacturing sector, which employs both skilled and unskilled labour, can provide the platform for resolving some of these issues. Writing on India's industrial policy, Niranjan Rajadhyaksha[65] noted that "the Asian experience tells us that no country can banish mass poverty unless it creates millions of new jobs a year in manufacturing and services". After interviewing an executive of the respected Indian Planning Commission, he concludes that "the goal of India's industrial policy is jobs". In the article "What happened to Ghana?" Simon Baptist, the Chief Economist of the Economist Intelligence Unit, compared South Korea's transformation and Ghana's performance. He stated that "the causes of South Korea's transformation are better known than the reasons for Sub-Saharan Africa's relative stagnation: good quality basic education, high savings, foreign investment, less corruption, and critically export manufacturing." He stated further that "there are virtually no countries that have transitioned from low income to upper middle income status without developing a vibrant export manufacturing sector." It is therefore not simply manufacturing but manufacturing that meets international standards, which forces manufacturers to upgrade their technology, and "raise their levels of value addition". There is strong evidence that exporting is linked to higher productivity. IMF research concluded that African firms that export are 17 per cent more productive than those that do not. Incidentally, in order to do this, Africa must deal with the question of a lack of skilled workers and an uncertain business environment, and governments must realign the incentives manufacturers face through a strong partnership that addresses manufacturing and export obstacles.

Growth in the manufacturing sector occurs when entrepreneurs increase their demand for innovation or increase their appetite for investment. Quite often, increasing this demand requires direct government actions. Fareed Zakaria[66] quoted an American CEO advocating government support for industry in a Time Magazine article on manufacturing policy as saying that "innovation doesn't just happen in laboratories by researchers, it happens on the factory floor." I agree. In fact, what happen in the laboratories are inventions, and it is the factory and the market that confer innovation status on those inventions. How can inventions be moved rapidly through the factory floors in order to address Africa's urgent need for jobs? Governments can help with this by enacting a strong industrial policy that is targeted and focused, and that builds on what is already in place with an industrial regime that monitors both the incentives provided and the performance of the targeted sectors.

The Nigerian Case

The Nigerian economy grew at a fairly decent rate of around 6-7 percent for the years before 2015. By all accounts, this is an impressive growth rate, indicating that the various regimes have done the right thing. However, the country's poverty rate—measured by those living on less than USD2 a day, according to a 2014 World Bank report is about 60 percent of the population, with unemployment remaining a very critical issue. According to the 2010 poverty survey of the National Bureau of Statistics has 61 per cent of Nigerians living under USD1 a day with the most conservative estimate putting unemployment at about 25 per cent, with youth unemployment at over 30 per cent, with 1.8 million graduates entering the labour market[67]. In presenting a recent World Bank report on Nigeria, a senior official said, "The issue we have in Nigeria is not unemployment but underemployment because most Nigerians cannot afford not to work, but a large share of the population is engaged in low productivity and low-paying tasks."[68] These two critical dimensions of our job market, low productivity and low wages, partly explain the pervasive poverty in our land, creating a large pool of the working poor. Poverty is both an urban and a rural phenomenon, with a higher incidence in rural areas. It may be worthy of note that life expectancy is 55 years in Nigeria, 65 in Ghana, and 76 in Brazil.

Nigeria's Manufacturing Gap and Rising Informal Sector

In this section, I shall rely on a 2014 detailed report on the Nigerian economy by McKinsey & Company.[69] The manufacturing sector, my main focus, has been growing at 13 per cent per year from 2010-2013, but at USD 35 billion, contributed only 7 per cent of GDP in 2013. Compare this to earlier data on manufacturing's contribution to GDP of more than 25% in countries where structural change has occurred.

We must place on record that 13 per cent per growth in the recent period is very impressive because, with the exception of China and Vietnam, such growth rates in manufacturing value added are difficult to maintain over a long period in a large economy. With a low manufacturing base, the positive externalities that flow from industrial technological upgrading and innovation are denied to the larger economy. With low and rudimentary technology in use, low productivity and low wages become the norm.

Mckinsey reports that "at less than USD 10, 300 per year, Nigerian output per worker is 57 percent less than the average of seven large developing countries: Russia, Mexico, Malaysia, Brazil, South Africa, and Indonesia". In manufacturing, the gap becomes even more glaring. Output per worker in manufacturing is USD5, 200 in Nigeria and USD 27,000 in South Africa. In addition to the technological gap, infrastructural deficits and low skills partly explain the difference. [Basic literacy among 15- to 24-year olds is 66 per cent in Nigeria, compared with 99 percent in South Africa]. It is therefore important that the enabling conditions for technical change, technology transfer, and, for that matter, the industrial revolution required to uplift many out of poverty include a solid educational base and appropriate incentives for the manufacturing sector that are founded on a strong partnership between the state and the private sector.

It therefore continues to baffle me that the Ministry of Science and Technology in Nigeria, a key ministry for any meaningful transformation, continues to be marginalized. If the new industrial revolution plan is to work, the Ministries of Science and Technology, Education, and the National Planning Commission must be assigned central roles. They must bring their assets to bear on the targeted sectors. Just like in South Korea, the industrial revolution was multi-sectoral, with the Korean Institute for Science and Technology and the National Planning Board playing key roles. An industrial revolution plan for Nigeria cannot be a Ministry of Industry plan.

The High Cost of Informality

According to McKinsey and Company, there are 32 million Nigerians employed in largely informal microbusinesses, with an average of 1.9 employees. For a very long-time, African governments and African intellectuals, including Nigerians, have romanticised the informal sector. Policies were geared to promote it, and very little was done to nudge these businesses towards formalisation. As a matter of fact, formalised businesses were increasingly cascading down into the informal sector, to avoid the rigours of the formal economy and engage in informal labour practices.

But informality comes at a huge cost to the economy. Informal businesses, by their nature, do not have the capital for technological upgrading and other investments in facilities that would raise labour productivity, hence wages that would lift the employees out of poverty. The report from McKinsey states that, "in countries with high informality, it is rare to see a strong cohort of fast growing small and mid-sized businesses that have access to capital and can drive job creation, productivity, and innovation". This high level of informality in the manufacturing sector is also contributing to the sector's low productivity. More importantly, these micro-enterprises are unlikely to have the assets and capacity to engage in export manufacturing, which has been the driver of poverty reduction in emerging economies. Unfortunately, some large businesses in Nigeria, including manufacturing businesses, have been engaging in informal behavior, hiring casual workers to avoid contractual obligations, with low wages leading to low commitment and low productivity. Owners of capital may benefit, but these acts cannot provide meaningful employment, which would have included formal and on-the-job training, skills upgrading that are the prerequisite for lifting those engaged out of poverty.

There have been several government interventions that have been targeted at the micro, small, and medium enterprises. These schemes must recognise and deal with the issues raised above. In our quest to tackle poverty, we have tended to think that small is better. Large indigenous enterprises in Nigeria, just like large scale-farmers, require assistance too. Large-scale manufacturing enterprises with assistance can be monitored to provide stable jobs, better wages, and better working conditions. Even the Federal government's ad-hoc internship programme relies on large formal enterprises. The South Korean experience teaches us that their focus on large-scale manufacturing was not misplaced.

We must ask, why did we not build our new automotive policy around indigenous firms such as Innoson Motors and others that have taken the risks; that are struggling with "first mover disadvantages" and infrastructural deficits, and create a system of innovation that would support the value chain around the industry? Such support would include research and development, marketing, a reduction in import bottlenecks, the development and deployment of targeted skilled manpower, the development of an ancillary supply chain, including critical parts that are currently imported, and the deployment of other smart subsidies from what Arthur Lewis calls "intelligent government". Unless you target a vehicle that is truly made in Nigeria and meets export standards, the full benefits of industry innovation and high tech will not translate into high productivity and high wages for Nigerians employed in the industry. That is how to structure an "economy built to last."

We must, therefore, resist the temptation to always apply federal character deleteriously in our economic policies in a manner that is harmful to the overall growth of the economy, and may even be anti-poor. When planned well, the growth of a particular region can act as a pull for the other regions. For instance, China has three city groups as economic growth poles: the Yangtze River Delta, the Pearl River Delta centred on the cities of Guangzhou and Shenzhen, and the city group around the Bohai Sea; a fourth one is being planned. According to Chinese Scholars, Lin Ling and Liu Shi-Quin of the Sichuan Academy of Sciences, China's development strategy prioritised the development of the eastern region, which contains these three growth poles. But these Eastern growth poles, according to these academics, have made great contributions to the economic and social development of China. The fourth pole being planned in the West is intended to achieve balanced and coordinated regional development around the country.

Given the centrality of planning for balanced and inclusive economic growth, a recent report regarding the intention of the government to privatise the Bank of Industry and the Bank of Agriculture is worrisome. These two banks are important for strategic industrialisation, manufacturing growth, and meaningful transformation. Privatization is likely to derail these objectives if profit-making becomes the central objective of these two institutions. There are other creative ways of re-capitalizing these two institutions to deliver targeted and cheap capital to the industrial and agricultural sectors.

The Problem with Nigeria's Federalism[70]

Another reason for Nigeria's growth without poverty reduction is the absence of "competitive federalism" and poor government accountability at the state and local level. With very few exceptions, Nigeria's states depend on the allocation of federally collected revenues that are distributed monthly. Because of this dependence, state governments often act as if they have no responsibility for any economic activity at the state level. Governors are not judged on the number of jobs they have created, the quality of the schools and the health care system, or the poverty rate within the state. As a result, states in Nigeria have not served as "engines of national prosperity" or "centers of economic and policy innovation" in the way American states have, as described by Bruce Katz.[71] Nigeria's federalism needs to be reformed. Immediately after independence, the country's states were actually quite competitive in social service delivery and economic activity—each exploiting its comparative advantage and contributing to national prosperity. However, with the success of Nigeria's oil industry, the states have become dependent on government revenues from the oil sector. As a consequence, the sense of competition among Nigeria's states dissipated. This needs to change. The federal government must take a leadership role and use its resources to promote good political and economic governance at the state and local level. It has to create a new incentive structure and a platform for performance evaluation without being hamstrung by the constitutional separation of powers. Additionally, each state's potential for economic diversification must be supported.

The states should be encouraged to work with the private sector towards the resolution of the many factors that inhibit diversification and the establishment of a manufacturing base around a particular product or commodity, i.e., "clusters." In some states, these clusters already exist, making it easier to address their needs. This is where future intervention by the international community, coordinated by the Nigerian government, should be directed. Eventually, they can be used to provide a strong platform for linking the agricultural transformation agenda and the industrial diversification agenda.

Another reason why Nigeria's states play a critical role in reducing poverty is because they are the entities responsible for primary and secondary education. Public schools in Nigeria are often of poor quality and unable to provide youth with the necessary skills for future employment. Consequently, many parents, if they can afford it, decide against sending their children to them, which widens the country's inequality gap as the children of the rich and middle class become better educated outside the public system and ultimately are better able to exploit future economic opportunities as they arise.

Shared economic development not only raises incomes, but it also raises the voice of citizens, their political participation, and their ability to demand government accountability. Poverty weakens citizen participation, which in turn exacerbates poverty. Nowhere in Nigeria is this lack of voice more evident than in the relationship between citizens and their state and local governments. Thus, diversification through manufacturing would not only raise incomes, it would hopefully lead to more civic participation and a demand for accountability. In pursuing what may appear as essentially an economic agenda, policymakers should realise that it has political and civic dimensions, which themselves have huge implications for poverty reduction.

Finally, growth is important. But the drivers and sources of this growth are equally important and need further interrogation. Inclusive growth and a permanent structural economic shift require diversification, especially in manufacturing. But diversification is not a natural phenomenon. You must cause it to occur. It requires the active intervention of a government—a purposeful government with visionary, value-driven leadership working in close partnership with entrepreneurs willing to create a society that cares, especially for the less privileged. The sort of partnership Obama acknowledged in his 2012 State of the Union address in relation to his government's opportunistic investment in positioning the manufacturing sector for the future, stating that, "in three years our partnership with the private sector has already positioned America to be the world's leading manufacturer of high-tech batteries."[72] Thus, some of the elements of the new industrial policy for which there is an emerging consensus include the following: that current assets cannot be a limiting factor to economic diversification; that a glorious future can be created through targeted investments involving public-private partnerships; that active government intervention is useful in helping to resolve complex quality assurance, supply chain difficulties, and knowledge requirements of the private sector. We hope that African leaders and those advising Africa will explore and encourage these partnerships and opportunities.

Finally, from Denis Waitely, Speaker and Author, "There are two primary choices in life: to accept conditions as they exist or accept the responsibility for changing them." I hope that we shall be part of the change we desire.

CHAPTER EIGHT

Aba: A Potential Engine of Prosperity and Her Knowledge and Physical Infrastructural Imperatives[73]

Yet, we speak of diversification in this country as if it will ordinarily occur. If we want it, the leadership must have the right policies driven by the right attitude to cause it to occur

1

When I was invited to speak on the infrastructural imperatives for the development of Aba as a centre of entrepreneurial excellence in the context of Abia State's development, I hesitated, even dithered, and came close to rejecting the invitation. To start with, I wasn't sure whether there was anything new I could add to the over-flogged issue of infrastructure for development. This has become the daily lamentation of Nigerians. Besides, I have not been to Aba recently and do not have first-hand knowledge of the current happenings sufficiently to be able to diagnose her salient problems and stand before you to proffer intelligent solutions. It is also not something that cursory research, even though I tried, could resolve.

On a second look, with broader lenses, I realised that those who framed the topic must be concerned about a lot more than the topic suggests, as many of us are. And Aba, an industrial city at the heartland of eastern Nigeria with thriving, autonomous clusters in clothing and shoemaking, is important for Nigeria's industrialization and for the goods it supplies to the West African region.

Permit me, therefore, to motivate this discussion by starting with why I think we are all gathered here. As you already know, How?" and "Why?" are important questions that need to be asked in the right order; it is impossible to decide how to do something effectively unless you can get to the heart of why you are doing it.[74] It is the most important question to ask before any individual or team embarks on any assignment. Why gets to the heart of the matter, and from it, certain solutions begin to emerge.

So why are we here? We are here because you are concerned about the history of our society, which has been characterised by both progress and decline. As the scholar F.J. Teggart taught us, history is plural, allowing us to evaluate every event with respect to the advancement it brought to individuals or society and the decline that same event may have brought. Aba typifies both advancement and decline, both promise and missed opportunity. The emphasis of the historian would depend on his or her ideology and the particular perspective or "determinative" he/she wants to elucidate. I also know that the group that has organised this lecture and all of us are concerned with the current processes that have brought Abia State or any other state to its current status and how we need to strengthen the structures and institutions with the supportive norms and values that have advanced other societies.

I recognized, like most of you do, that we must construct a dialogue that forces us to discipline ourselves in order to confront those actions, values, allures, traps, and extreme individualism that have tended to benefit a few and set our communities into decline. The fact that you have an Abia Think Thank Association with notable people indicates that you are willing to go against our selfish gene. This is even more so when our politics and economy are organised to set these traps and allures and to promote anti-community values. So, we are concerned about building Aba as a centre of entrepreneurial excellence, but we are even more concerned about building a society where individuals are able to resist these selfish temptations; for as Aristotle said, "I count him braver who overcomes his desires than him who conquers his enemies; for the hardest victory is over oneself." Having the character and the discipline of mind for moderation, deriving happiness from hard work, self-knowledge, building relationships with others, pursuing and accepting political responsibilities based on ethics, promoting the good of all, and creating what Jeffrey Sachs refers to as a [75]"mindful society" must be why we are gathered here. In his book, The Price of Civilization, Prof. Sachs states:

> There are many errors in the libertarian philosophy, but the biggest of all is its starting point: that individuals can truly find happiness by being left alone, unburdened by ethical or political responsibilities to others…Happiness arises not only through an individual's relationship with his wealth, as some economists simplistically

assume, but through his relations with others. A society of compassion, mutual help, and collective decision-making is good not just for the poor, who may receive help, but also for the rich, who may give it. (Sachs, 2011, p.163).

There is, therefore, an enlightened self-interest being pursued when we gather as we have gathered here to enlarge the democratic and policymaking space; when we align our individual moral responsibilities to the creation and sustenance of the common good and the eradication of poverty, we are creating a "mindful society". I am hopeful that that is why we are discussing Aba. What would be the essence of promoting Aba as a centre of entrepreneurial excellence? Is it to pursue unbridled individual wealth, show off more, and disconnect from the rest of society, or is it to use Aba as a wealth and technological engine for the advancement of all Abians, all Igbos, and indeed all Nigerians and humanity? The Abia Think Tank Association is appealing to the state and federal governments to help it become an active participant in the market place for ideas. The state and federal governments of Nigeria have not done well in expanding the space for informed policy debates and in partnering with think-tanks to pursue ideas for development. And this is not new. Government policies are mostly driven by the civil service. In very limited instances, new policies may be the result of the initiatives of a few reform-minded ministers or commissioners or governors. But they usually lack expert guidance and are clearly devoid of civil society and broader input from the citizenry. When expert advice is sought, we have also seen some irksome tendencies to rely on powerful interests and external sources that may not share our values, anxieties, risks, or aspirations. What the Abia Think Tank Association is doing with this lecture and other activities of this nature is to seek for active engagement through dialogue and to increase the avenues for citizens to be part of the resolution of critical policy issues. And in the process, promote democratic governance, enlarge economic participation, and create "the mindful society", where trust is built and collective engagement shapes future progress that would, hopefully, benefit the majority.

In discussing Abia's development and Aba as a hub for entrepreneurial excellence, I know that you are reflecting on the larger society that berths her spirit of enterprise and technological innovations, beckoning to be harnessed and governed. I know that you must understand what politics does to economics and the spirit of excellence in our clime, *underscoring the superiority of politics over economics*. I also know that you are worried about how insecurity and state planning, or the lack thereof, affect the progress of this undeveloped hub. I know that as Abians, you are ashamed about the decline in Aba and that your collective wisdom has not been tapped to remedy the situation. And I have been apprised of some of the efforts being made by the state to resolve some of these issues. One can only encourage them to be systematic, persistent, and knowledge-driven. Short-term measures create mediocrity, opportunity for half-baked, reversible solutions that tantalise the citizenry without having any lasting impact on their lives.

I know that in the end we will declare or restate that in order to create a "mindful society" where enterprises such as those envisaged for Aba would thrive to be globally competitive and wealth would be created for the advancement of Abians and Nigerians, we would also need a mindful state and a mindful government.

2
Aba as a Catalyst for Structural Change and Diversification

I now turn my attention to the phenomenon that is Aba and the nature of its infrastructural imperatives. First, Aba is important for Abians, for Ndi-Igbo, and for Nigerians. This is an indisputable fact. The gift of Aba lies in the fact that while other states and countries worry about the creation of innovation clusters or hubs, Aba emerged endogenously without assistance from anyone. The wonder that is Aba comes from the enterprise spirit of the citizens of Abia state and this region, and the bare-knuckled struggle of our brothers and sisters who put their imaginations to great purpose, using "a potent combination of constraints and ambitions to ignite a new genre of innovation"; learning to do more with less and navigating the many infrastructural deficits that many in their situation in emerging countries take for granted. It appears that the more constraining the environment, the more innovative they have become. But there is a limit to how far these enterprises can go without a supportive state. Those who collapsed under the weight of this poor support may have suffered much, if not more, than those who found a way to survive. Aba is indeed a gift waiting to be harnessed, scaled up, and formalised to the benefit of entrepreneurs, government, and society.

In a concept note on Funding Issues for Infrastructure, Prof. Melvin Ayogu and I identified infrastructure as including both physical and social infrastructure such as highways and roads, mass-transit and airport facilities, education and health facilities, electricity, gas, and water supply facilities and distribution systems, waste treatment facilities, correctional institutions, police, fire service, and the judiciary. When you discuss infrastructure for Aba, there is a wide array of facilities and systems to consider. Roads and electricity are important, but so are the rule of law, an independent judiciary, good health facilities, and an effective police force. Most of these are factored in when investors, especially foreign investors, are evaluating investment options. Core infrastructures, comprising highways, water, electricity, and telecommunications, are extremely important because they enter directly, as intermediate inputs into private-sector production or even aggregate production activities. These components are expected to contribute most directly to private-sector output. You can see why we might be concerned about Aba's infrastructure. As with any public good, some benefits of infrastructure capital, such as improved security, time savings from better roads and/or reliable telecommunications, improved health, and a cleaner environment, are of magnitudes that are difficult to measure and thus value in monetary terms. But they are important.

Given the large-scale involvement of governments in infrastructure investment, evidence from Prof. Ayogu's research has shown that the patterns of growth in infrastructure stocks are better explained by political economy than by economic efficiency. How else can we explain the neglect and decline that is Aba? Infrastructure for Aba cannot be a constituency project. It cannot be a project that waits for similar *Abas* to emerge in six geopolitical zones so that we can be seen to be fair to all zones. This attitude of treating all zones equally in all situations undermines the national vision, national identity, planning and any sensible national development strategy. Aba and Nnewi represent the South East economic zone and their manufacturing activities are easily linked to the hides and skins and cotton production in the North and the ICT hub in Lagos in the South-West. The

Chinese three economic city groups: the Yangtze River Delta, the Pearl River Delta centred on the cities of Guangzhou and Shenzhen, and the city group around the Bohai Sea; and a fourth one is being planned captures appropriately how economic development can be prioritized above political consideration. According to Chinese Scholars, Lin Ling and Liu Shi-Quin of the Sichuan Academy of Sciences, China's development strategy prioritised the development of the eastern region, which contains these three growth poles. But these Eastern growth poles, according to these academics, have made great contributions to the economic and social development of China. The fourth pole being planned in the West is intended to achieve balanced and coordinated regional development around the country. Thus, Aba is a federal government concern, South East governments' concern, Abia State government's concern, the concern of the private sector and all of us concerned with the development of Nigeria. I believe that if the governments of the South East see the zone as an economic zone, with Aba and Nnewi as focal economic cities, their combined efforts will garner more attention from the Federal government. The Abia Think Tank Association now has a role to champion this cause and explain to all the states how they would all benefit if Aba became the economic pearl of the east. The governments must realise that the benefits from investing in infrastructure in Aba, in terms of future revenue accruing to both the states and the federal government, can be immense if the activities of the entrepreneurs are upgraded and formalised, not to mention the multiplier effects of job creation and the creation of a "mindful society". I cannot overemphasise the critical importance of the formalization of these businesses for growth, learning, and inter-generation transfer. The current family-owned model and the apprenticeship system have serious limitations. While it has served us well in the past, it will require modernisation and institutionalisation for this great system to survive.

The widening inequality of our time, as we see growth in the economy with rising poverty, can, in my view, be attributed to the manufacturing gap in the economy and the absence of structural change. In chapter seven, I made this argument very forcefully. I indicated that Nigeria's manufacturing contribution to GDP is less than 5 percent. Compare that to Brazil (20), China (34), Malaysia (30), Thailand (35), and Indonesia (28). These are countries where structural change has taken place, and they are the same countries that are lifting millions of their citizens out of poverty. According to Dani Rodrick, a Harvard University Professor of Economics, [76]"development is fundamentally about structural change," and I agree. He continues, "The driving force for economic development cannot be the forces of comparative advantage as conventionally understood. The trick seems to be to acquire mastery over a broader range of activities instead of concentrating on what one does best." For as long as we neglect Aba and other potential manufacturing hubs, we will continue to depend on the export of primary commodities and on import of finished goods.

But, Dani Rodrick and many other economists, including myself, know that mastery over a broad range of activities, especially those with value addition that leads to diversification is not a natural process. Yet, we speak of diversification in this country as if it will ordinarily occur. If we want it, we must cause it to occur. Here is Aba, a manufacturing hub that yearns to be a catalyst for structural change but has lacked the support of what Arthur Lewis calls the "intelligent state" required to resolve its "first mover disadvantages" and complex innovation challenges that are often beyond the capacity of an individual or group of entrepreneurs. In essence, in Aba we are describing enterprises whose owners have demonstrated willingness to take risks with "great social value" and have, therefore, already invested in what Hausman and Rodrick call "self-discovery." They have taken those first bold steps that are critical and have also demonstrated what is possible.

Positioning Aba as an Innovation Hub

Aba needs good roads, uninterrupted electricity, an adequate water supply, and a clean environment. As important as these are, I would like to emphasise the importance of knowledge infrastructure within a national or subnational innovation system. This is absolutely lacking in Aba, and anything remotely resembling it is so informal and insignificant. First, definitions and concepts: According to Professor Freeman, a national or sub-national system of innovation would refer to "the network of institutions in the public and private sectors whose activities and interactions initiate, import, modify, and diffuse new technologies". It is the interaction of institutions and actors in the public and private sectors as they generate, import, adapt, and adopt technologies for strategic developmental goals (my modification). Technology-led development is a leadership endeavor. Presidents John F. Kennedy, Lee Kuan Yew, Fidel Castro, and Olusegun Obasanjo are great examples of leaders who understood the importance of science, technology, and innovation and led from the front. And Aba is a technological hub. But it is a hub without the supporting infrastructure of a system of innovation.

Infrastructure, especially knowledge infrastructures such as vocational schools, polytechnics, universities, libraries, ICT systems, broadband availability, are critical in upgrading Aba from an enterprise zone to an innovation hub. But they have to be organised around the production structures, with specific roles assigned to specific actors and the state acting as an intelligent broker. Without Aba being an innovation hub, it would be impossible to reap its full potential. What is lacking is the co-evolution of Aba as a production centre and a knowledge center—creating a dichotomy between what Aba people know how to do and what they should learn to do to be internationally competitive—and what the various governments should do in terms of institutional and knowledge support to improve the learning process. Through the application of incentives, including patenting and licensing, the state is able to support a wide-ranging application of ideas, technology, and innovation that may have emanated with a private actor. [Talking about patenting, I have often wondered why we expect our Herbalists and traditional medicine experts to give us their knowledge for free when they hold uncommon knowledge that is patentable or that is a common community resource. If you pay them handsomely, they will have the incentive to release their knowledge. This is the basis of patenting.]

What am I really saying? For the enterprises in Aba to grow and be internationally competitive, we need to surround Aba with relevant vocational schools, a polytechnic, and an engineering department that can supply the knowledge required to improve the efficiency of their production processes, force backward integration, promote specialisation, and scale up production. Then you would need a government agency that can steer things up – like an Aba Technology Development Agency [ATDA] or Aba Industrial Development Agency. This quasi-government agency would be led by key figures from the private sector, with the goal of improving the outcomes of Aba's innovation cluster for the benefits of the people of Abia State, South East and Nigeria. Those who govern the territory where Aba is located must have a certain attitude and important knowledge and ideology to drive this ambition. This is currently lacking.

The State as a Broker: Examples from Finland and the United States

It was the government of Finland, through an agency called TEKES that brokered the emergence of the Nokia phone. Ordinarily, Nokia started off as a rain boot manufacturer and moved up to electrical insulator manufacturing. With the state's brokerage role, Nokia became a major player in the telecommunications industry. The story of Finland is very interesting because Finland, just like Nigeria, was a resource-based economy, exporting paper as part of its forestry products.

Nokia became a national product.

In 2000, Nokia contributed

- ❑ 2 percent to the GDP growth rate
- ❑ 35 percent of the total R&D
- ❑ 20 percent of exports
- ❑ 1 percent of total employment
- ❑ In 2007 contributed 23 per cent of all Finland taxes

These data are dated, but they illustrate the point.

The State of Arkansas, a small basically rural state in the United States, established an Arkansas Science and Development Authority (ASTA).

It runs a number of small programmes to support ST&I for the state

- ■ Applied research grant programme
- ■ An R&D tax credit programme
- ■ A seed capital fund
- ■ Technology development and transfer programmes
- ■ Priority areas include: advanced materials; agriculture; food; manufacturing systems; transport; and logistics

These areas of focus were well laid out through strategic mapping of priorities, opportunities, and strengths. The outcome was that the Arkansas economy added nearly 46,000 jobs from 1998 to 2000, with the largest number in mid-wage industries including construction, transportation, wholesale trade, and manufacturing. The information industry grew by 10 per cent and auxiliary business services grew by about 30 per cent. It is evident that when an intelligent government and the private sector collaborate, the economy grows in a more inclusive manner.

President Barack Obama, in his 2012 State of the Union address, was emphatic that manufacturing must return to America because it is fundamental to "an economy built to last." In this address, he underscored the importance of the partnership between the state and the private sector. He stated, "it is public research dollars, over the course of 30 years, that helped develop technologies to extract all this natural gas out of shale rock… government support is critical in helping businesses get new energy ideas off the ground". Many scholars have always characterised America's use of public resources to support industry through public funding of R&D as subsidy by another name. If Africa's manufacturing sector is to grow, it requires a smart and market-friendly industrial policy built on a partnership between the state and the private sector. The type Obama talked about in his address when he stated that "in three years, our partnership with the private sector has already positioned America to be the world's leading manufacturer of high-tech batteries." That is America, the leading industrialised nation in the world, explaining how the government assists the many private sector breakthroughs. Why hasn't Aba caught the attention of our various governments in a very special way?

We return to Aba. If, for the sake of argument, we limit Aba as an enterprise zone known for the production of apparels_(shoes and clothing), it means that we must be training people in footwear and clothing design; in tool maintenance and retooling; in improving production; in business processes; in book-keeping; in sales; etc. It is no coincidence that Italy is the world's design capital. It has well-established institutions, including design colleges that are world-class. Even South Africa has several colleges that support their clothing and shoe industries. They have a Footwear Design and Technology School in South Africa that started in 2009. It has now expanded to Cape Town, Pretoria, Durban, and Johannesburg. I would like to challenge the Abia Think Tank to think of ways to start a private polytechnic that supports the manufacturing concerns in Aba. This can be linked to the proposed Aba Industrial (Technology) Agency. Such a polytechnic would train students on business processes, standards and quality control, design, materials technology, machine maintenance, product and sales training, etc.

The need for backward integration is also critical. Aba is a mature enterprise zone in apparels. Why is it that all its raw materials are basically imported? Nigeria exports hides and skins to Italy, where Aba imports leather. Almost all its wool is now either from China or Italy. The processes required for partial or full integration are often beyond what an individual entrepreneur can undertake; hence, the call for the state to broker access to machinery, technology, and experienced teachers from elsewhere.

The Need for the Establishment of an Inland Port in Aba

This backward integration is linked to the creation of an inland port in Aba. The existence of such a port would increase the competitiveness of Aba products; the port as a centre of transshipment would reduce import and export costs and facilitate easy storage and consolidation of goods. It may require road and rail infrastructure. An Aba inland port is an idea whose time has come. Kenya has inland ports in Eldoret, Kisumu, Embakassi, and Nairobi. Ghana has in Kumassi, and Uganda in Torroro and Port bell. All of these ports have been set up to support their enterprise zones.

As Malcom X said, "education is our passport to the future, for tomorrow belongs to the people who prepare for it today." With education, a new attitude, a new orientation, the political will, and an intelligent government, we shall realise the Aba of our dream.

CHAPTER NINE

How Do You Create a Resilient Nigerian Economy?

The supreme reality of our time is our indivisibility as children of God and our common vulnerability on this planet, President John F. Kennedy

I have heard a couple of senior members of the current Nigerian government speak about how they are setting out to create a resilient economy. At the 2016 World Economic Forum in Davos, a few persons also spoke about nurturing a resilient economy. None of the speakers elaborated on the elements and parameters of this resilience. In fact, it looked like a new cliché was in town. Not surprising, global instability has become the new norm. Every country is now grappling with how to cushion the effects of global instability on their domestic economies. The greater the size of your shock absorbers, the more resilient or less brittle you are. The richer, more developed countries have more sophisticated, more diversified shock absorbers than developing countries. Even though "the rich also cry", they have more sophisticated tools, skills, institutions, a strong national ethos, good politics, and knowledge infrastructure to reengineer themselves out of crisis faster than a developing country such as Nigeria.

But even they cannot claim that their economy is resilient. As we are beginning to see with the case of China, great economic success and excessive speed can wear out your shock absorbers, dilute your socio-cultural assets, and expose your vulnerability. But many African countries would welcome China's seeming dilemma rather than be in the doldrums that they have found themselves in. China's dilemma is not China's alone to worry about. Its slowdown has become our slow-down as well, as China demands less of what we and others produce. Human failure, greed, the desire to accumulate faster than my neighbour, and institutional and regulatory failure in America led to the global financial crisis of 2008 that spared no nation, degrading everyone's assets in its wake. A virus detected in one country can very quickly become an epidemic in another, very distant country. That is the nature of the modern world — a world of constant upheaval often triggered by an innocuous event, often without warning – an ecological disaster, a regime change, or major disruptions such as wars, terrorism, or sudden commodity price crises. In this interconnected world, how do you build a resilient economy? How do you build strong shock absorbers and circuit breakers that can isolate the problems, given the limits of human knowledge and foresight? If volatility is inevitable, how can we design a system that allows an economy to sail through the rough tides and re-adapt without the people losing their identity, socio-cultural assets, and purpose?

Economists have always known that sectors are interdependent and that policies must complement each other for a holistic solution. Hence, they know that the solution to an agricultural problem may lie in the health sector, the solution to a health problem may lie in the education sector, and so on. They also know that a certain fiscal policy, no matter how well-intentioned, can undermine the attainment of the objectives of even the most robust monetary policy if they are decoupled. The economist has been taught how to gather information and the right data, analyse it, appreciate the big picture, and draw important macroeconomic lessons. The coupling of sectors and policies and the need for analysis that paints a holistic picture force the economist to think before he acts and to theorise before he practices. In short, this process underscores the limits of common sense and the inherent danger that is associated with partial solutions.

And I see this danger daily. Commentators, opinion-formers, politicians, and businesspersons of all shades, after disclaiming that they are not economists or even social scientists, engage in partial analysis and proffer partial solutions. Partial solutions are bad enough because they can create significant problems within the same system. However, they are exacerbated when "incubated in the dark," guided by body language, inured by our selfish or ulterior motives, guided by street-level analysis rather than deep reasoning, with exaggerated fear or unwarranted optimism. But economists also know that their tools are limited and that globalisation, "the mother of all coupling processes—connecting nations, markets, corporations, and events; with human and non-human systems—technical, financial, and even ecological—interacting and producing feedback loops that may be delayed or that proceed at a speed that has never been anticipated before"[77], has diminished the predictive power of their trade, if they had any. On the matter of resilience, you require a deeper and more sophisticated way of thinking about constructing shock absorbers, adaptive capacity, and how to recover from upheavals. This is beyond economics and certainly beyond market determinism[78]. Economists should therefore eat the "humble pie" and come to the table with humility.

In search of answers on how to construct a resilient economy, I turned to an innovative, very accessible new book by Andrew Zoli and Anne Marie Healy titled, you guessed it, Resilience[79]. Borrowing from sociology and ecology, the authors define resilience as "the capacity of a system, enterprise, or person to maintain its core purpose and integrity in the face of dramatically changed circumstances." Key parameters of resilience are, therefore, "continuity and recovery in the face of change." In the book, we are guided to understand that in building a resilient economy, it is critical to ensure that all parts of the economic system are invested and linked in a complementary manner, so when disruptions occur, the various parts of the system can react to create stability. This would require new laws and institutions—strong and credible institutions that tie the hands of leaders —in order to allow the institutions to pursue their short-and long-term objectives. But the benefits of these laws and the activities of these institutions must be "tangible and clear to all stakeholders in a transparent manner." If the Central Bank is independent, it must be seen to be independent in reality in the pursuit of its core mandate and cannot be operating under the shadow of political and other considerations. However, the Central bank must have the right information, data, and analysis as well as must apply the right science. And there are other national critical institutions, such as the Bureau of Public Enterprise, whose decisions, activities, and actions continue to come under increasing scrutiny, sometimes at great cost, because they don't meet the resilient test of "transparency and accountability to all stakeholders". Having the right institutions and institutional effectiveness is, therefore, key to resilience.

There are a few other issues that need to be addressed in Nigeria in order to build a resilient economy. Resilience comes from diversification—be it diversification of the revenue base, diversification of the economy, and input sources; blocking of revenue leakages; anti-corruption measures; and a disciplined workforce. One cannot build a resilient economy in an economy where corruption is pervasive. The current anti-corruption drive is well-placed. But it must be pursued within a framework that provides for punishment and reward, incentives for the right behavior and disincentive for the wrong behaviour. It is a long-term fight that must entrench rule-based behaviour and value reorientation. The fight requires exemplary courage, strong leadership, and building a strong coalition for change. But this fight should also address the apparent rot in the state and local governments. Transparency and accountability as a driver of inclusiveness, shared prosperity, or equitable sharing of not-having are one of the bedrocks of a resilient economy.

Diversification of the economy away from dependence on oil into manufacturing and industry is not a natural phenomenon. It does not come from policy pronouncements. It comes from a coordinated and concerted implementation of intelligent industrial policy that is targeted at some goods and services, relying on both static and dynamic comparative advantage. Such a policy is also cross-sectoral and led from the top. It comes from the resolution of current coordination failures and the realignment of critical relevant national institutions. It comes from the production of solid graduates in Science, Technology, Engineering, and Mathematics whose skill sets, aptitude, and attitude are geared towards the production of diverse goods and services. It comes from engineering an innovation economy with strong science, technology, and innovation infrastructure. If you interrogate the current national budget, it becomes clear that diversification, as a core objective of government, is still treated at the level of generality. It comes from a coordinated approach to infrastructure development that appreciates the complementary roles of the public and private sectors in an intelligent Public-Private-Partnership (PPP) framework that provides quality services and protects consumers. In short, diversification comes from a multi-year national plan that anticipates tomorrow, targets short- and long-term goals, and is not constrained by the politics of now. Such a plan must depend more on our internal resources than external borrowing in order to minimise our vulnerability to eventual unsolicited policy advice and conditionality from international institutions, and our subsequent dependency and loss of policy autonomy. But how can there be a national plan without a sense of a nation? Any diversification that is not built on this solid foundation, which does not flow from a plan and a coordinated approach, cannot withstand any upheaval, be it from human, ecological, political, technological, or international market stressors.

In diversifying the economy and revenue base for the country, we must re-engineer and restructure the states as industrial and innovation hubs and sources of autonomous revenue for deepening development. The current overdependence on federal allocation increases the nation's vulnerability because the component parts are not "invested and linked in a complementary manner". Resilience requires the sharing of the burden of development among the several tiers of government, with regional or state plans complementing national plans. I find it rather sad that the federal government is saddled with the responsibility of primary education, as the proposed feeding of primary school pupils confirms. The National Economic Council, rather than acting as a forum for how revenue from the federation should be shared or improved upon, should be a platform for discussing the industrial competitiveness of the states, their social programmes, their complementarity to one another, their strengths and weaknesses, and how to improve their business environment and economic partnership with the federal government in a more strategic way. Diversification is key to building a resilient economy, but it should not be the sole responsibility of the federal government.

And there is more. Creating a resilient economy requires the building and nurturing of informal social, cultural, and economic networks to tap into the connection between tradition and modernity, scientific and social, formal and informal governance, including traditional institutions, cooperatives, and non-governmental organisations. These institutions, when linked and nurtured across states and regions, can be a source of knowledge exchange, economies of scale, additional sources of capital, especially for small and medium enterprises (SMEs), national cohesion and integration, and can create additional shock absorbers in times of volatility. But networks are built on trust—social capital. And trust is built on the right values. Right now, there is both a trust and value deficit in Nigeria. Resilience will require a fundamental re-orientation of our values and work ethics; the deconstruction of aspects of our culture; de-biasing the populace with their pre-conceived notions of one another, raising of critical minds that elevate our dialogue, challenging untested assumptions and what is otherwise taken as "manifest destiny" that have held us back and led to complacency. And complacency is antithetical to resilience.

Above all, creating a resilient economy necessitates charismatic leadership with grace: a leader who can enlarge the tribe, the Nigerian tribe; a leader who is both discerning and detailed; a leader manager who can delegate but supervises; who values both macro and micro perspectives; and who can drive good politics (for bad politics leads to bad economics that corrupts any resilient feature of the economy). Zolli and Heally describe such a leader as translational. According to them, such a leader "has the ability to knit together different constituencies and institutions, brokering relationships and transactions across different political, economic, and social organisations... seamlessly working up and down and across organisational hierarchies, connecting with groups who might otherwise be excluded, and translating between constituencies."[80] These leaders "derive their authority not solely from their formal status but from their informal authority and cultural standing" – integrity, the ability to create shared values, and a symbol of national cohesion. But translational leaders are needed at the national, state, and local government level as well as at the community levels. This calls into question our political leadership recruitment process that has been, thus far, not development focused.

There you have it: resilience requires our coming to terms with the fact that volatility is the new norm and would require all of us joining hands, making the necessary sacrifice, approaching development with a new attitude and thinking and acting differently in order to build an economy with improved shock-absorbers.

PART FOUR
Development and Insecurity

CHAPTER TEN

Economic Inequality and Insecurity

Where justice is denied, where poverty is enforced, where ignorance prevails, and where any one class is made to feel that society is in organised conspiracy to oppress, rob, and degrade them, neither persons nor property will be safe, - Fredrick Douglas, Washington, DC, 1886.

In the words of a Nobel Prize winner, Armatya Sen,

Poverty and economic inequality may not instantly breed terrorism or influence the leaders of terrorist organizations, but they can help to create rich recruiting grounds for the foot soldiers of the terrorist camps.

1
Inequality and insecurity—the absence of a "mindful society"

My thesis is that it is not poverty per se that creates insecurity. Economic inequality, the growing gap between rich and poor, breeds insecurity. It creates an unfair and unjust society, leaving many in a state of hopelessness. Relative deprivation created by an unfair economic system and poor governance that feeds the exploitative class—both business and political—to the detriment of the poor is a significant recipe for insecurity. In other words, when we were all poor, insecurity was not an issue. We were all safer. Insecurity became a natural result as the commonwealth became increasingly private and captured by a few.

With great advances in technology, life is supposed to be more abundant and meaningful for all. And indeed, the world, including Nigeria, has generated enormous wealth. With civilisation and enlightenment, and with our shared history and common humanity, we are supposed to be more accommodative and tolerant, more inclusive in the sharing of prosperity, and we are supposed to have conquered our primordial instincts of survival of the fittest and primitive accumulation. But we have not. Historically, violence and insecurity were associated with struggles for control of scarce resources. While the struggle for control of scarce resources still exists as we sometimes see in "just and unjust wars", the more dangerous forms of insecurity, as we experience them in Nigeria, have arisen as a result of widening structural or systemic inequality created by unbridled greed, selfishness, poor governance by the ruling elite, poor attitudes of the business elite, and the absence of a "mindful society". A mindful society resists the lure of mass consumerism; a mindful society cannot be ranked number one in the importation of champagne while ranking number one in under-five malnutrition; a mindful society is concerned about the poverty trap of many of our working poor. It seems, therefore, that with technology, new knowledge, and creative business ideas, life has become increasingly abundant for the few, as those who command this social means of production are increasingly appropriating the massive benefits privately. While technology is promoting interconnectedness and "social intercourse between nations and peoples" through the internet and electronic and social media, it is equally polarising the world as the benefits of the knowledge and technological world are shared unequally. Access to and control over knowledge and technology have lost their moral and socialising value.

When I was growing up, the children of *Oga's* driver attended the same school as the children of *Oga* (the master or wealthy class), providing a level playing field and equal opportunity.

Right now, the children of *Oga* are all schooling in the very expensive private schools in Nigeria or abroad, whereas the children of the driver are left in dilapidated public schooling where there is schools without learning, breeding an army of unemployables. Injustice is reigning supreme. It is a world where our freedoms as citizens of the world are curtailed by the "non-citizen" actions of kidnappers, armed robbers, cultists, Boko haram members, suicide bombers, and other fringe groups that are equally destroying the basis of their citizenship. But they don't care. It is a world where justice and equity deficits are creating hopelessness and misery, forcing young people to see the state as the enemy and every successful person as an oppressor. But many have been misled to wear the garb of violence in the mistaken belief that it is the means to create hope, justice, and equity. Worse, the guise of violence is increasingly being painted with a new religious paint, with adherents being indoctrinated to see every non-adherent as an enemy and a legitimate target. Violence affects the perpetrator. Insecurity hardly discriminates among its victims. Therein lays the greater danger. Suddenly, your friend and neighbor becomes a target; your fellow traveler chained by the same yoke of injustice becomes a target; ordinary citizens, passengers in an aircraft, a group in a church, mosque or market become victims of weapons of mass destruction in the hands of brain-washed religious zealots and, used and discarded political miscreants.

2
Greater Equality, Strong Citizenship and Societies

Greater equality makes for more accountable and caring citizens, according to Richard Wilkinson and Kate Pickett in their seminal book.[81] In the book, they ask: "Why do Americans mistrust their fellow citizens more than the Japanese do? Why do Americans have higher rates of teenage pregnancy than the French? Why do Americans have more homicides than the Spanish, Australians, and Danes put together? And the answer: America has greater inequality!"

I can ask the same questions about Nigeria. Why is there such a massive lack of trust in Nigeria among citizens and between citizens and their governments? Why do we have kidnapping, terrorism, banditry, and rising prostitution? Why do we have one of the highest maternal and infant mortality rates in the world? Why are our students in school but barely learning? Why do we have one of the highest numbers of children out of school? Why is it that domestic violence, rape, and gender inequity are rising in our society? Why do we have rising insecurity? Why are our political processes bedeviled by thuggery and mediocrity? Why are we now a nation of endemic corruption? We can find the answers in our widening inequality. The situation is exacerbated by our growing economy, which makes a few very rich and the majority very poor, and this is complicated by inter-and intra-regional inequality. which leads to wide disparity in capabilities, undermines our patriotism and sense of oneness, and hoists a new set of wrong values on us, with everyone scheming to undermine our laws and institutions, with poorer segment of the society dialectically challenging the same laws and institutions that are supposed to protect them, unfortunately without necessarily advancing their own agenda or improving their situation.

All around the world, from Asia to Europe, from the Arab world to North America to Africa and Nigeria, inequity and injustice reign, fueling all forms of non-peaceful coexistence and, sometimes, extremist behaviour, often of the violent variety. And this is not to excuse violence and extreme behaviour because violence is an unintelligent and incompetent response to social injustice. But it is to recognise how acts of omission or commission that diminish any one's or any group's human dignity—from a rigged election to dictatorship; from corrupt leadership to incompetent or insensitive leadership; from racial to religious bigotry; from economic structures that benefit a few disrupt the tenets of peace. According to Mahatma Gandhi, poverty is one of the worst forms of violence. And we have governments that have, over the years, carried on with policies and acts that continually impoverished her people and hoped that all the armies and police of this world would help them maintain peace.

In the foreword of the aforementioned book, The Spirit Level, Robert Reich, a Professor of Public Policy at the University of California at Berkeley, stated that "inequality undermines the trust, solidarity, and mutuality on which the responsibilities of citizenship depend." Simply put, inequality breeds lawlessness and irresponsible citizenship. So how can you have responsible citizens where there is one law for the poor and another for the rich? And the penalty for a small breach of the law by the poor is swift and severe, but the rich are allowed to use technicalities to escape the long arm of the law. How can you have mutuality and solidarity when every rich Nigerian man dies in London or Paris and every poor man dies in his forsaken village or urban slum?

3
Inequality and Insecurity – The Need for Holistic Solutions

So, if the prevalence of ill health, capability deprivation, crime, and other social problems are related to inequality, why has this problem remained intractable even in advanced economies? In addition to relying on the market that, in many instances, created the problem to reverse the problem, Wilkinson and Pickett point out that many of the policy initiatives pursue partial solutions, and attempt to "break the links between socio-economic disadvantage and the problems it produces". In pursuing partial solutions, policymakers often assume that the circumstances of the poor do not matter as long as the issues they are confronted with are dealt with one by one. However, every issue is linked to another. So, what is required is a holistic solution that addresses the circumstances of those who have found themselves at the lower end of the socio-economic rung, with states (not only the federal government) recognising that they must become centres of shared prosperity.

So, it is not about *tradermoni,*[8283] or such like schemes and palliatives. It is about giving the poor a stake in the economy now and in its future. The poor will need to improve their knowledge and capabilities in order to be an active participant in the economy. It means access to good public education and health facilities. It is about stimulating inclusive growth by undertaking stable and transparent macroeconomic policies; growth that is induced by an intelligent state providing incentives for domestic and foreign investment in the employment-generating sectors, increasing credit to agriculture by encouraging large-scale farming to improve agricultural productivity; using research institutions to support the generation of knowledge and technology for the productive sector; increasing the productivity of the poor through access to technology and knowledge; expanding the manufacturing sectors by directing development banks to advance credits to strategic import substitution manufacturing; taming inflation; and controlling population.

When you expand economic opportunities through-reform induced growth, how can you spread these new possibilities and make them inclusive? I turn to Amartya Sen and his insights in his book, *Development as Freedom*[84]. According to him, "many Asian economies – first Japan, and then South korea, Taiwan, Hong Kong, and Singapore, and latter post-reform China and Thailand...have done remarkably well in spreading the economic opportunities through an adequately supportive social background, including high levels of literacy, numeracy, and basic education; good general health care; completed land reforms etc. In other words, raising the capabilities of the poor, addressing their "capability poverty" in all its ramifications must be seen as complementary to economic growth if growth is to become inclusive. Policies must therefore address the many *"unfreedoms"* associated with poverty and inequality in order to have any significant impact on insecurity. You need to raise the productivity of the poor by raising their human capital assets; provide a level playing field, and incentivise productive engagements in rural areas.

But these solutions must emanate from a developmental state with developmental institutions that extend and tame the market economy—institutions that address the ethical behaviour of society, that build trust and reorient values, that are concerned with the redistribution of wealth, and that have a fair and progressive tax system that taxes the rich to provide services that the poor enjoy. We require institutions that moderate the incentives for the unbridled pursuit of private rather than social goals; institutions that produce politicians and policymakers who understand and are willing to use their economic and political space to pursue common goods and agendas. We need to support growth with a revised developmental ethic, realising that in the long-run, widening inequality would undermine economic success.

4
Insecurity, Youths and Existential Vacuum

As for the youths, the situations we have created have left many in search of meaning and purpose for their lives. In his book, Man's Search for Meaning, Victor E. Frankel talks about the "existential vacuum" as "a wide-spread phenomenon of the 20th century" arising from the loss of animal instincts; that paradise of freedom that allows us to label most behaviour as arising from instinct. This is coupled with another loss arising from the absence of a dominant culture that prescribes the boundaries of behaviour and determines how we ought to behave. So, we are left unguided, not relying on our primitive instincts, and not bound or disciplined by culture. This would not have been an issue if this phenomenon was benign. But we are now forced to make choices, good or bad, as knowledge beings and enlightened humans. It is this existential vacuum that leads to aggression, suicide, rape, and other off-limit, extreme, and often dangerous behaviour. What have we done to contribute to this existential vacuum that now exists, especially among our youth? It is not simply that we have lost our instincts and dominant culture of control, but that our actions, policies, activities, and personal conduct are creating this existential vacuum for our youth. What hope is there for the future of the youth when teachers do not teach, governors do not govern, ministers do not minister, leaders do not lead, and parents do not parent, and preachers preach hate instead of love? Many of our young people are, therefore, still searching for meaning in their lives, leading to a poor perception of themselves and alienation from society that has conspired against them. If unchecked, the search for meaning can make someone, especially a youth, susceptible to drug abuse and recruitment into violent-prone brotherhoods and affiliations—cultism and the like.

Finally, if we realise, like Bono did in the foreword to Jeffrey Sach's book, The End of Poverty[85], that "the destinies of the "haves" are intrinsically linked to the fate of the "have-nothing at alls", we must learn to govern differently at all levels and aspire to create a just and less exploitative economic system. We must understand that the war against insecurity should be a comprehensive war against poverty and, more importantly, a comprehensive approach to creating a caring society and reducing inequality. The task is for competent governments with the right attitude to set a clear strategic direction and boundaries, and for the private sector to key in.

CHAPTER ELEVEN

Curbing Insecurity in Nigeria: The Imperatives of Inter-Security Agency Collaboration and Co-Ordination

Advice is a stranger; if he's welcome, he stays for the night; if not, he leaves the same day. – Malagasy Proverb

Whenever I am invited to speak on any topic, I usually start by probing the motive behind the choice of the subject in relation to the goals of the institution that hosts the lecture. It helps me to situate the lecture; allows me to recognise and appreciate the institution for bringing to the fore a key problem that has obviously been of concern; to applaud their disposition in allowing external insights to be brought to bear on the problem; and, finally, it allows me to acknowledge my knowledge-gap.

Introspection requires courage. Inviting someone, an external agent, to look in takes even more guts because you never know where the pestle of responsibility and accountability will land. I, therefore, salute the leadership of the army for the courage it displayed in pursuing this enlightened self-interest and in inviting me, an academic, to share my thoughts on this important subject of intelligence coordination and collaboration in the context of our deeply troubling, evolving, multi-dimensional insecurity challenges. In inviting me, you are asking me to bring my perspective, hopefully an intelligent one, to the subject of this lecture. For that is indeed all that I have. For I have no military or security background, but I have a well-trained social scientist's perspective with a diverse intellectual orientation, grounded in a proper ideological focus and undiluted patriotism. In the end, I hope that we can conclude with resolution and the resolve to change the situation. And that we don't suffer from what Greek philosophers call *akrasia*, the weakness of the will to pursue the right course of action.

In addressing you, I will be addressing all other arms of our security architecture, the political leadership at all levels, all other stakeholders embroiled in the search for answers, and, indeed, the entire nation. I have never believed that any problem can be addressed solely through a circumscribed prism that yields quick and often sub-optimal partial solutions. You would, therefore, permit me to dig wider and deeper into the human and institutional failures that are the root of many of your problems and our problems. In this search for the truth, I might inspire and embolden you to search for answers yourselves, or castigate and caution you to release the knowledge and experiences that lie inside the Army as an institution and change your ways and those of other sister institutions in order to create the desired outcome for yourselves and for the greater good of our society. We are encouraged by the teachings of the synoptic gospel[86]:

> If you bring out what is inside of you,
> What is inside of you will save you.
> If you fail to bring out what is inside of you,
> What is inside of you will destroy you.

Today's engagement reminds us that the military is an enlightened and disciplined institution that is frequently looking for intelligent solutions to its own immediate problems while also caring deeply about societal needs. But what we are currently faced with goes beyond the issues of discipline, knowledge, and enlightenment. If truth be told, we are confronted with institutions that the populace is not satisfied with. And that is not all. There seems to be an equal disenchantment among the providers of these services about their institutions and the services they provide. Pardon me, but looking from afar, it seems that no one is satisfied, not the army or the security institutions and their clients. If we were, there would have been no need for this lecture, and there would have been no clamour for alternative security architecture. We learn from the book, Practical Wisdom,[87] that it is easier to do the right thing (pursue goals and meet expectations) when everyone around you is also so inclined. And "more likely, when your institution encourages and nurtures doing the right thing". This is not to provide the army an escape route; their behaviour must mimic that of society. Not at all. I recall my university colleagues attempting to make a similar argument at a retreat: that the university, and thus the behaviour of lecturers and others, is a reflection of society. I disagreed. I implored them to understand that the university is where the rest of society comes to learn how things should be done. The gown dictates the pace for the town to follow rather than the other way round. Similarly, the army is the epitome of discipline, organisation, strategy, goal orientation, high morale, and patriotism. Society is supposed to learn these attributes from the army. However, what is the reality? Are the goals set by the political masters clear? But let us not get too far ahead of ourselves. We shall return to these issues later as we examine the fundamental questions around the subject of this lecture and the human and institutional discontents.   Nothing said here will diminish the appreciation of Nigerians for the sacrifices all of you in the security services make. The nation is grateful.

2
Insecurity in the Context of Equity, Justice, and Development

To be secure is to enjoy protection from all forms of physical harm or loss of legitimate property, freedom from threats and the anxiety that danger looms, and the preservation of your way of life and values. Development—the qualitative improvement in the living conditions of citizens—presupposes that security is basically guaranteed. It is for this reason that the Constitution of the Federal Republic of Nigeria, Section 14(1)(b) states "that security and welfare of the people shall be the primary purpose of government". There is a reason security was placed before welfare. If the citizens are to enjoy a certain level of welfare, well-being, or civilization, they must first be secure and feel secure.

In addition, while a secure environment is necessary for development and the welfare of our citizens, there are un-welfare issues; other unfreedoms that cause insecurity and are a result of the political, economic, and social decisions made by our leadership and systems. In his pathbreaking book, Development as Freedom, the Nobel Prize Winner, Amartya Sen, identified other unfreedoms: unfreedom from ignorance, unfreedom from hunger, unfreedom from a healthy life, unfreedom from political participation and public voice, etc. These ill-gotten freedoms feed directly into insecurity. Ignorance feeds directly into what Professor Sen identified in another book, Identity and Violence,[88] "a single identity syndrome". According to him, it is this "singular affiliation syndrome" that forces these perpetrators of violence to "ignore altogether all other linkages that could moderate their loyalty… and to ignore all affiliations and loyalties other than those emanating from one restrictive identity …and how this can be deeply deceptive and also contribute to social tension and violence". I am Igbo, a Nigerian, a Christian, a Catholic, a father, a husband, a teacher, a researcher, a banker, an economist, a politician, a Rotarian, and a Paul Harris Fellow. So, who am I? How can you target me because of a single identity and ignore my other affiliations, which are equally important? In the community of teachers or Rotarians where I also belong, there are Christians, Muslims, Hausas, Yorubas, Tivs, Ibibios, Hindus, and even atheists, blacks, whites, and Asians, and we enjoy common bonds as teachers and Rotarians. But this is the result of ignorance, which is fueling violence all over the world, in Nigeria, (old) Rwanda, other parts of Africa, old Yugoslavia, America, and so on why is the education of the populace not a priority for the ruling class—education that gives everyone a basic understanding of our common humanity?

Poverty is the greatest source of unfreedom, and Mahatma Gandhi characterised it as one of the worst forms of violence. But crime, hence insecurity, is more directly related to inequality. And inequality is a political and economic choice. Nations that are more equal produce stronger and more secure societies. If in doubt, look at the Scandinavian countries- Sweden, Norway, and Denmark. When we were all poor, we were relatively more secure. It is not surprising because inequality weakens the camaraderie and patriotism upon which accountable citizenship is built. The emergence of non-state violent actors is, in part, a result of a sense of not being a stakeholder in the Nigeria project now or in its future. And make no mistake about it, external aggressors have home-based collaborators. No one will destroy a country in which he has a stake or knows that his children will be active beneficiaries of its future prosperity. In 1886, the American civil rights advocate Fredrick Douglas captured what I am trying to say in these indelible words, that "where justice is denied, where poverty is enforced, where ignorance prevails, and where any one class is made to feel that society is in an organised conspiracy to oppress, rob, and degrade them, neither persons nor property will be safe".

But we are now dealing with more than crimes. As we deal with organised crime and terrorism, for that is what banditry and all other forms of criminality we suffer in Nigeria are, we must acknowledge that crime is a product of a lack of capacity to apply moral restraint, in the calculus of risk and reward in favour of reward, the absence of a suitable alternative, and other predisposing environments or situations. So, there is the psychological experience of the person or persons involved resulting, in part, from their social and economic circumstances (basically limited opportunity) interacting with prevailing circumstances such as under-governed spaces, porous border, the influx of small arms and light weapons, ideological brainwashing and ignorant interpretation of what the different civilisations stand for, and poorly equipped, motivated, and undermanned security forces.[89]

We acknowledge that violence is an unintelligent way of expressing dissatisfaction with a system, but we must acknowledge that these fundamentals are critical in understanding our insecure environment and the search for a wholistic solution. It is useful to understand why these organised criminals have collaborators, informants, and logistic suppliers without regard for national harm when looking for community intelligence or intelligence coordination. It is also important because certain aspects of insecurity are beyond the scope of core military activities. More importantly, the preceding discussions inform us that the insecurity problems must be framed correctly if effective solutions can be adduced, either within the agency or inter-agency. Political correctness or calling something what it is not is likely to hamper intelligence gathering and sharing, speed of logistics deployment, morale, and organisational effectiveness. A doctor must first properly diagnose and name the disease before treating the patient. Otherwise, the treatment would be a patch of guesswork and may be in vain.

3
The Multi-Dimensional Nature of Insecurity in Nigeria

Insecurity is evolving in Nigeria and changing in nature and character. Its many dimensions are also location-specific with some significant overlap, indicating that the crisis is now more pervasive than previously thought. They include the Boko Haram insurgency, unusual herdsmen-farmer clashes, armed and criminal herdsmen, armed robbery, kidnapping for ransom, militancy in the Niger Delta and

South East, piracy and oil theft, cattle rustling, unknown gunmen (a strange phenomenon), and banditry. The killings, maiming, and disruptions to the social and economic lives of Nigerians arising from these organised crimes are staggering. Unfortunately, it is not subsiding. I don't want to bore you with figures, but let's illustrate the point with the consequences of bandit attacks. Between 2018 and 2020, an estimated 4900 people lost their lives; 309,000 internally displaced people and 60,000 refugees have been recorded. According to the United Nations Development Report, Boko Haram has caused up until 2020, 35,000 direct deaths and 314,000 indirect deaths. For every one death, nine children, especially those under the age of five, die from hunger, malnutrition, and lack of resources. But these figures do not tell the full story. How do you quantify the sit-at home in the south-east every Monday, ordered and enforced by unknown gunmen? The perception of Nigeria as an unsafe investment destination worsens our current economic crisis and further creates an environment that feeds insecurity.

In all of these insecurity types, with their emerging and dynamic dimensions, security intelligence gathering is at the heart of the solution. To allow non-state actors this level of "free-ride" in terrorising citizens is a failure of security intelligence. More specifically, it is pointing to a significant lack of cooperation and coordination among the many security agencies charged with keeping Nigerians and their properties safe. It is also pointing to a lack of capacity, human and institutional failures.

4
Security Architecture and Intelligence Coordination and Its Discontents

The following agencies have intelligence gathering and processing capacity, and in many, it constitutes the main objective:

National Intelligence Agency (NIA), State Security Service (SSS), Nigeria Police Force (NPF), Defence Intelligence Agency (DIA), Directorate of Military Intelligence (DMI), Directorate of Naval Intelligence Agency (DNIA), Directorate of Airforce Intelligence (DAI), Nigeria Immigration Service (NIS), Nigeria Customs Service

(NCS), National Drug Law Enforcement Agency (NDLEA), and Nigerian Security and Civil Defence Corps (NSCDC). With this many agencies, one would expect top-notch intelligence gathering for effective national security, but not if they act in silos. It is envisaged that the Office of the National Security Adviser (ONSA) would be the collation point for both internal and external intelligence and that the office would have the responsibility for transmitting the intelligence to the appropriate agency for immediate and timely action.[90] So, a coordinating role is envisaged for the ONSA. But how effective is this coordinating role? What level of authority does the NSA have over the service chiefs and heads of other agencies that have supervising ministers. Is the coordination established by law with appropriate powers or is it an ad-hoc arrangements that did not envisage the pervasive and complex security situation Nigeria currently faces? In other words, what has changed in both personnel and institutional arrangement to reflect the current reality? Are there clear objectives and goals that all the agencies subscribe to and that are transmitted to them? Bear in mind that divergent goals not only create significant difficulty in inter-agency collaboration, they also make-upon agreed policies difficult to implement, requiring inevitably a "more formal cooperation process" among the agencies.[91] Is there, therefore, a new intelligence architecture that promptly processes the data, reducing the reaction time, and prevents events before they occur? In this architecture, are there crime-specific groups (committees) for the deepening of knowledge around a particular crime and its evolving nature? In other words, do you have a group focusing on banditry and another on kidnapping or Boko Haram-type? Specialised knowledge is now required to address specific crimes.

I have read several books (accounts) about how Osama bin Laden was apprehended and killed. Each account details the significance of inter-agency intelligence collaboration; the importance of data gathering and expert analysis; the use of technology and human agents for data gathering; the definition of objective by the President; the focus of a particular group of intelligence experts on this assignment; the top-secret nature of the assignment; the leadership that was provided at the highest level; the resources that were made available to the patriotic team; the diligence, the frustration suffered and overcame. The intelligence process was detailed, competent, and painstaking. It was only the military action that was swift.

In search of answers to these questions, I turned to the National Security Strategy 2019[92]. I read through a robust document that covered the various aspects of national security, including economic and social dimensions, but did not devote any section of the strategy to inter-agency intelligence coordination. I felt that this was a major gap given that the fight against organised crime such as terrorism and banditry depends on the quality of the intelligence assets and how these assets are coordinated. In the report (p. 21), it states in one sentence that the strategy proposes a "viable technology-enabled intelligence infrastructure" without any elaboration. In another section of the report, it states that "internal security is the responsibility of all Nigerians, but it is the statutory duty of a large number of security and intelligence agencies in Nigeria. However, the Joint Intelligence Board (JIB) and the Intelligence Community Committee (ICC), working in concert with the National Crisis Management Center (NCMC), will continue to coordinate intelligence and information analysis required for strategic decision making by the National Security Council". I was excited at the existence of JIB and ICC, but the document was silent on their coordinating roles and did not state whether they were institutions created to increase the operational efficiency of the intelligence community in a harmonised manner. In other words, the document in this respect lacked specificity in terms of their leadership and assignment of responsibility. I may be wrong, but this was my ordinary reading of this section of the strategy. So, where is the framework for joint inter-agency coordination?

In another section, it states that: "To prevent the incidence of kidnapping, armed banditry, and militia activities, we will proactively activate systems for early warning and early responses established in the national crisis response mechanism. We will address disputes and conflicts through regular dialogue by exploiting traditional faith-based and state structures of peace building and alternative dispute resolution before they trigger crises and violence." At this point, I was lost. The proposed solutions were not only vague; I wasn't sure whether they were still addressing kidnapping, armed banditry, and militia activities. Furthermore, I kept asking myself who "We" is in the document. I suspect that the strategy may have suffered from what many national strategy documents suffer from. Rather than being truly national, it is often the product of one ministry or agency, reflecting the aspirations, goals, and modus operandi of the origination or coordinating agency without any significant input from other stakeholders. I did not give up. I was elated to see a sentence that states that "to improve the overall effectiveness and efficiency of intervention measures, we will develop doctrines for inter-agency coordination and collaboration." Unfortunately, I did not see any framework that could give one an inkling of what the doctrines would look like. Whether this was ever developed, this audience can confirm it better than I. Please remember that this lecture is not supposed to be a critique of the national security strategy. This is what you in the military call collateral damage. It was the search for answers to the earlier questions that led us to the strategy document. Unfortunately, the questions remained significantly unanswered. I am only providing my own perspective.

We are now left to search for answers in the literature[93]. Inter-agency cooperation within the security intelligence architecture in Nigeria will be enhanced by the following: the goals must be shared across agencies (goal congruency is not limited to inter-agency; it is also extended to the goals of the political masters); capacity to gather and analyse intelligence data must exist across agencies (this is important for reliability); resources, both for capacity enhancement and as an incentive for cooperative behaviour, must exist both centrally and across agencies; the command and control structure of coordination must be clear and unambiguous, the subordination of the different philosophies of the various organisations into one philosophy established by the political masters for goal attainment is required. Leadership with character and the assignment of competent personnel into the right roles (devoid of politics, nepotism, and excessive adherence to federal character must be the norm, the standard operating procedure; in this matter of life and death, federal character can take a back seat. Let's deploy the best that we have. And they are there).

The Human Elements that have Hindered Security Intelligence Coordination[94]

These elements include: (i) Rivalry among the security forces due, in part, to overlapping areas of responsibility; (ii) mutual distrust; (iii) the feeling of superiority of one over another engendering envy and jealousy; (iv) acts of indiscipline due to poor education, superiority complex, ignorance that weakens "spirit de corps"; (v) corruption and use of resources for other purposes; (vi) poor remuneration; (vii) unhealthy rank comparisons; (viii) ineffective command and control due to organisational failure (perhaps absence of enabling law) and weak leadership; (ix) poor inter-service communication hinders effective intelligence gathering, sharing and speedy operationalization among the agencies; (x) inter-agency struggle for operational funding.

It is important to note that embedded in the identification of the problem are the solutions. But broadly, the solutions revolve around: (1) institutional configuration and realignment (perhaps with a new law) for formalisation of relationships; (2) competent leadership with character; (3) capacity building and training for both hard and soft skills; (4) adequate resources, remuneration and other morale-boosting incentives, including adaptation, devolving authority to junior officers who may be more creative and innovative; and (5) political will (with clear goal definition). It also requires: planning together, reviewing the plans together, training together, and building relationships through retreats. The joint task forces often set up at the sub-national levels are useful but have not been effective in stemming the spate of these organised crimes. Partly because these state ad-hoc institutions lack effective command and control, and the governor's authority to force cohesion among the agencies as the Chief Security Officer of the state can be easily undermined. It means that there are gaps that need to be evaluated and remedied.

Lessons from Other Nations

Lack of adaptation and public accountability among senior officers bedeviled some of the wars that America engaged in, resulting in huge losses in human and material resources. According to some analysts, this is due to a lack of alternative voices in the military as well as a lack of political leadership (civilian) access to the debates in which the military participates. Out of frustration, a US Army Lt. Col. Paul Yingling wrote an essay in 2007 stating, "We have lost thousands of lives and spent hundreds of billions of dollars in the last seven years in efforts to bring stability to two medium-sized countries; we can't afford to adapt this slowly in the future… the problem is that a private who loses a rifle suffers far greater consequences than a general who loses a war". [95]

What can we learn from Israel, a nation that is in a constant state of war in this respect? The Israelis are constantly and publicly evaluating their war efforts, "hearing testimonies from angry army officers about the government and the military's conduct during the war". In the view of Israelis, the second Lebanese war was botched. According to retired General Giora Eiland, former head of the National Security Council[96], "open-minded thought, necessary to reduce the risk of sticking to preconceived ideas and relying on unquestioned assumptions, was far too rare". Continuing, he said, "one of the problems of the second Lebanon war was the exaggerated adherence of senior officers to the chief of staff's decisions." All these meant that there was no flexibility, creativity, or innovation. One wonders whether Nigeria's current fight against insecurity is suffering from inflexibility and excessive hierarchy in the security agencies? Are you sacrificing "flexibility for discipline; initiative for organisation; innovation for predictability"; and a successful outcome for authority? Do security agencies in Nigeria allow junior and middle level officers to interrogate strategies and make contributions, as in the Israeli model, or are they simply required to obey and implement? What intelligence gathering role has the military assigned to the department responsible for the military-civilian interface in the deployment of soft power? Large institutions such as the military and other security agencies must be cautious of "groupthink, sycophancy, and submissiveness" to avoid huge mistakes and errors that would prevent them from constantly reinventing themselves, especially in the light of fast evolving security challenges.

Leadership Philosophy, Character and Coordination Failure

We cannot overemphasise the issue of character in leadership. It is critical to the success of all human endeavours and explains the human failings that make coordination very difficult. In the military, the issue of character must factor into intelligence and other command assignments, especially when the nation is going through these myriads of security challenges. When we make strategic postings such as that of the GOCs or other sensitive postings, is it simply based on rank or a combination of rank and character? What about promotions? But what is character?

> Character consists of valuing the good more than one's own desires, of being honest when dishonesty is personally beneficial, of exercising self-control when the impulse towards self-gratification is more powerful] – Dennis Prager

> Good character consists of recognising the selfishness that inheres in each of us and trying to balance it against the altruism (*idealism*) to which we should all aspire. It is a difficult balance to strike, but no definition of goodness can be complete without it.- Alan M. Dershowitz

> Leadership is a potent combination of strategy and character. But if you must be without one, be without strategy.
> General Norman Schwarzkopf, United States Army general who led the Coalition Forces to liberate Kuwait from Saddam Hussein of Iraq in 1991. {He would rather give command to someone with character than to one who is a master of strategy but without character}.

> It is not in the still calm of life or the repose (restfulness) of pacific stations that great characters are formed. The habits of vigorous mind are formed in contending with difficulty. Great necessities call our great virtues
> Abigail Adams, the confidant and wife of John Adams, the second President of the United States, 1780. {We know who is who when we are confronted with difficult situations. It is then that our character is exposed}.

There are at least six pillars of character: Trustworthiness (honesty, keeping your promise and being courageous to do what is right even in the face of difficulty); Respect (listen to what others have to say; be polite; deal peacefully with anger); Responsibility (think before you act, persevere and be responsible for your choices); Fairness (play by the rules, don't blame others carelessly, don't take advantage of others, and avoid tribalism and parapoism); Caring (be compassionate, show gratitude, and forgive others); Citizenship (be patriotic, respect authority, engage and facilitate others to engage in civic duties, vote, and pay your taxes).

If you take these quotes and the six pillars of character together, you would find answers to the myriads of questions we have raised. Coordination failure arises because of the weaknesses in our character. Whether it is ego problems, a superiority complex, insubordination, abuse of power, corruption, or the absence of political will, they all find expression in the weakness of character. Even when institutions are created to organize, incentivise, and sanction behaviour, people still find ways to subvert them for selfish and parochial reasons. Fix character, and you will fix coordination. Character building should be an essential part of all military, para-military, and security formations' training. Fortunately, character, like transformational leadership, can be learned. And bad behaviour and poor habits can be unlearned.

Inter-Agency Coordination Failure: Lessons from Other Ministries, Departments, and Agencies (MDAs)

But coordination failure is not peculiar to our security architecture. Part of the explanation for our economic and developmental outcomes is attributable to coordination failure. Many of the MDAs charged with implementing our economic policies act in silos and belong to different ministries with different goals and objectives. The appointment of the management and boards of some of the most critical parastatals and agencies does not reflect the knowledge or seriousness of the mandate of these institutions. Once ministers are in place, the overarching objective of national development, which coordination could reinforce, takes a back seat to power and turf protection. I bring this up here because there are parallels to our subject matter and lessons to be learned. Without prejudice, let's illustrate this point with the following institutions: The Nigerian Export-Import Bank (NEXIM) reports to the Ministry of Finance, the Bank of Industry reports to the Ministry of Industry, the Bank of Agriculture reports to the Ministry of Agriculture, and the Raw Material Research and Development Council reports to the Ministry of Science, Technology, and Innovation, and the Nigerian Ports Authority reports to the Ministry of Transport. These agencies are critical to the diversification of the economy and other economic agenda of the government of Nigeria. And there are many talented and devoted employees in these institutions. But who is coordinating their activities towards this stated goal? Even when it may be stated on paper, which institution or leader has the power to compel the other to act, to sanction one who is out of line, or to provide incentives for inter-agency cooperation? You are likely to find these important agencies working very hard but pursuing goals that do not add up to the stated overarching goal of the government because of coordination failure.

In a recent study on stemming international financial flows in Nigeria by notable experts,[97] a similar coordination failure among the agencies responsible for gathering intelligence and prosecuting criminals was confronted. He was looking at institutions charged with the responsibility of investigating and reporting on anti-money laundering and other financial crimes. Principally, they include, Central Bank of Nigeria (CBN), Federal Inland Revenue Service (FIRS), National Drug Law Enforcement Agency (NDLEA), National Bureau of Statistics (NBS), Nigerian Financial Intelligence Unit (NFIU), Nigeria Extractive Industries Transparency Initiative (NEITI), Federal Ministry of Finance, Independent Corrupt Practices and Other Related Offences Commission (ICPC), Economic and Financial Crimes Commission (EFCC). Interestingly, the report noted that "brain trust" was not lacking in these agencies given the depth of knowledge of the staff the author interviewed in the various agencies. He stated:

> Based on the extensive interviews and content analysis, the opinion of this report is that were officials in lead positions suitably empowered (i.e., incentivised, backed by political will, and the establishment of effective inter-agency cooperation) they can at the least substantially decrease the external outflow of illicit monies and contain the crime proceeds within Nigeria's jurisdictional

boundaries". He continued, "in the anti-money laundering crusade, it is becoming abundantly clear that securing inter-agency cooperation is indeed a mission-critical infrastructure... but agencies are apprehensive about extensive sharing of information because of leakage... but go on to recommend that it is possible to devise mechanisms that circumscribe this leakage concern". Other recommendations include: "commitment from the leadership to actualise the goal (without undue political interference), a functional interagency platform comprised of nominated agency personnel with executive powers can be forged—especially if agency heads are predominantly political appointees—using career high-level employees". The report also recommends institutional affiliation re-arrangement (for goal alignment) that can engender public confidence in the volunteer of intelligence and information.

I have done this extensive review on embedded lessons for the security architecture and intelligence coordination. I can bet that if a similar study is conducted among the security institutions with respect to intelligence coordination, the results would not be very different. There are knowledgeable and patriotic people in the system, but are they in charge? There is mutual suspicion that affects knowledge and information sharing. There is turf defense and leadership ego that obscures appreciation for the big picture. Above all, there are significant concerns and gaps around incentives, sanctions, acceptance of responsibility, inter-agency rivalry, and political will. Same issues that are likely to debilitate interagency coordination among the security agencies.

These lessons remind me of two African proverbs. The first states that "two birds tied together have four wings that cannot fly". You can only fly when your wings are not incapacitated. And you would fly further with the support of another bird. The second, a Kenyan proverb says, "It is not necessary for fingers to look alike, but it is necessary for them to cooperate". Each finger has a role to play in attaining their joint objective, irrespective of its size.

Coordination Imperatives and Institutional Realignment - Lessons from America

Institutions should be built around problems, essentially to have a coordinated focus on addressing the challenges currently being faced. When new and emergent threats occur and persist, it would not make sense to continue business as usual, or tinker with things at the margin, or be cosmetic with reforms. When Americans were confronted with externally and domestically inspired terrorism, especially after the September 11, 2001 terror attack, the Federal Government Created the Department of Homeland Security (DHS), through a Home Land Security Act of 2002. This was a coordinating agency. It brought twenty-two (22) government agencies into a single organisation, including US Customs Service, Immigration and Naturalisation Service, Transport Security Administration, Federal Protective Services, and many others concerned with the safety of American citizens at home. According to a political scientist, Peter Andreas, the creation of DHS constituted the most [98]significant government reorganisation since the cold war and the most substantial reorganisation of federal agencies since the National Security Act of 1947 (which created the National Security Council and CIA and placed the different military departments under a secretary of defense). You should note that these agencies came from different departments, and no one was fighting to maintain their turf or areas of operational influence. What was uppermost in the minds of policymakers and legislators was coordination and operational efficiency for the safety of Americans. Moving the US Customs Service from the Treasury to DHS reoriented the institution and changed its philosophy from a revenue agency to both a revenue and security agency, with great emphasis on security.

In the United States of America, there were also issues of "service parochialism", yet "jointness", the term used to describe team work, was promoted. Every great military campaign of the modern era has been a joint effort. But according to Collin Powel, in his memoir, My American Journey, "jointness in our time was more often produced out of the necessity of the moment than built into the military psychology." Consensus military advice, according to Powel, was built on "scratching each other's back – as staff spent hours searching for the least common denominator that was, in the end, found not very useful". This is to underscore that collaboration and coordination do not occur naturally. They are caused to happen. And when the United States was confronting a major security challenge, parochialism was jettisoned in the national interest.

There is also the role of legislation in strengthening existing institutions. For many years, according to Collin Powel in his memoir, the Joint Chiefs of Staff office was ineffective as a strong voice for joint advice to the President and the Congress. And the "failings", according to him "were more bureaucratic." He regarded it as an "amorphous set-up". There was the initial suggestion of setting-up a national military council with members who would have no responsibility for their particular service and could therefore devote their full energies to coordinating the armed forces. But this was regarded as an interim measure.

In 1982, General David Jones, the 9th Chairman of the Joint Chiefs of Staff, spoke out of frustration after his retirement. According to Collin Powel, "Jones recommended that the JCS Chairman becomes the "principal" military adviser to the Secretary of Defense and the President and be given greater authority over the staff serving the Chiefs". In response, there was the Defense Reorganisation Act of 1986, – championed by Senator Barry Goldwater and Congressman Bill Nichols. According to Powell, "this act gave the Chairman of the JCS real power – as a principal military adviser. He had the authority to give counsel directly to the Secretary and the President" without looking over his shoulders.

The important lesson here is that legislation can be used to improve military or security intelligence coordination and effectiveness. It can come in the form of a new institution, but it can also simply serve to strengthen existing ones. However, it implies that you have knowledgeable legislators who understand the patriotic roles they have been elected to play. And who can think beyond transactions, bringing some intellectual and analytical reasoning to bear on their duty, working with competent leadership of the security agencies in the national interest. The critical question is: what informs our selection of chairmen or members of the defence or other important committees of our National Assembly?

Conclusions

We have raised more questions than answers. I have provided my perspectives the best I can in the context of this lecture and the time constraint imposed by the short notice. But this has been useful. We need to encourage national public reasoning on significant national issues. We need to promote national solidarity among citizens and among all military and security agencies as we seek a secure environment. Peace and security require justice and equity in the sharing of the burden of development and similar equity in the sharing of the prosperity that arises from social and economic progress. Indignity, poverty, inequality, and a rising sense of national unfairness and exclusion undermine citizenship and other attributes of character, providing the environment for crimes to thrive and the recruitment of terror gangs.

The current spate of insecurity must shame us all. It is in the acknowledgement of this embarrassment that a heightened sense of national duty will emerge and positive outcomes will be obtained. But we cannot lie to ourselves. The political class must provide leadership and call the disease by its name. It is also their duty to define the strategic approach with clear command and control that forces collaboration and effectiveness. The military and all the other intelligence agencies must realise that there is strength in humility and that ego is the enemy of collaboration. Attitude adjustment is required at all levels of leadership and among the rank and file of the security institutions.

Coordination of inter-agency intelligence is an art, requiring high national morality, character, humility, diligence, innovation, adaptation, competence, incentives, institutional reconfiguration, strong ideology, values, and patriotism. It also requires targets, outcomes, and goals with strict consequences. We are all unhappy. It is our collective responsibility to change this state of affairs through the decisions and choices we make. What are you doing in your little sphere of influence? Can we all aspire to create islands of excellence in our work areas and in our duties. Together, we shall overcome.

PART FIVE
Development Strategies in the Face of Global Disruption

CHAPTER TWELVE

Managing the Nigerian Economy Post Covid-19
-Issues and Strategy -

1

The Nigerian economy was already facing serious economic and developmental challenges before COVID-19. Coming out of recession and growing at 3.6 percent against the population growth rate of 2.6 per cent in 2021, the situation was dire. Inclusive growth has eluded Nigeria even when growth rates were in the range of 6-7 per cent largely due to the sources of growth and the absence of intelligent, robust programmes and plans by the government (at all levels) to realign public expenditures for the effective delivery of infrastructure and social services and to provide direction to the private sector. Short-term and partial measures meant that critical foundations for improving productivity across all the productive sectors were neglected and job-focused industrialisation was not prioritised. With low productivity, real incomes were declining, and poverty was worsening. Nigeria's output per worker, according to a 2014 Mckinsey report, is 57per cent less than the average of seven large developing countries. The government's agricultural policy of putting more people and more land under cultivation, the policy of "extensification" instead of "intensification", underscores the absence of basic understanding that what is required is how to improve yield per acre and per capita food production. In the words of the former Prime Minister of Israel, Shimon Peres, "Agriculture is 95 per cent science and 5 per cent labour". This fact is often lost on our policymakers, who are often not problem-solving oriented. This low productivity across sectors, especially in agriculture, will become an issue in the management of the post-COVID-19 economy.

Nigeria's urbanisation has been somewhat atypical because, rather than contributing to raising productivity, it has contributed to its low productivity trajectory because urbanisation has not followed industrialisation. Most of the urban dwellers are underemployed, and many eke out a living in the informal sector. There is a huge cost to informality. Increasing informality has negative consequences for GDP per capita growth. With this informality increasing and being encouraged, the likelihood of the emergence of structured small and medium business outfits with access to capital and potential for innovation, job creation, productivity, and tax revenue diminishes. The absence of an urban-based manufacturing sector is a major factor contributing to Nigeria's increasing poverty. The strategy for formalising the informal sector into medium enterprises and in supporting the emergence of a more robust manufacturing sector would be critical for a prosperous and resilient post COVID-19 Nigerian economy after COVID-19.

The government sector was already under serious stress before COVID-19. The overreliance on oil revenue often makes both national and state budgets precarious and unimplementable. Yet, the budget is a major instrument for managing the economy and serves as a signpost to the private sector and international business as to the direction of government policies. There is very little fiscal space because debt service is now over 120 percent of total revenue and the excess crude account – savings for the rainy day- has been drawn down. The projected tax revenue of over 8.5 trillion Naira by the Federal Inland Revenue Service is now a mirage. With constant fluctuations in the global oil price regularly invalidating the budgets of federal and state governments. This also coincides with the government's implementation of the Minimum Wage Act. With very little room for borrowing, now is the time for a truly homegrown structural adjustment and an opportunity to construct an economy without oil. It would require institutional and policy coordination, rationalisation of public assets, and strict accountability. This is no time for partial solutions or partisanship. But this will require discipline, capacity, political will, transparency, and the bridging of trust-deficits.

2

Managing the Post Pandemic Economy and the Opportunities

Two major areas of immediate and long-term concern:

1. Health
2. Economy

i. Health

I will not dwell much on the health sector except to make a few comments. First, COVID-19 has exposed how fragile and weak our health institutions and systems are, both at the national and subnational levels. The reliance on foreign treatment by the elite has shielded them from the true picture of things. President Buhari missed an opportunity to be a champion of homegrown, robust health infrastructure when he returned from a 100-day treatment abroad. He could have tapped into the national sentiment and sympathy to engineer a public-private sector partnership that would have given Nigeria one or two world-class hospitals. This Pandemic has provided another opportunity for the president to initiate and engineer this, tapping into domestic philanthropy, high net-worth individuals, the business community, and Nigeria's medical diaspora. But more importantly, the states must be incentivized by the federal government to come up with plans to revitalise the public health sector in their states. These plans will place great emphasis on public health, public health education, nutrition, and the management of infectious diseases with the appropriate expertise and infrastructure. The same PPP arrangements can be replicated in the states given that the economy would not be able to support huge public expenditures at this time. Prior to COVID-19, Nigeria faced serious hygiene and sanitation challenges, as well as malaria, tuberculosis, malnutrition, maternal mortality, and Lassa fever. Other challenges include limited access to quality care, poor service delivery, and brain drain. These challenges would remain and could get worse post-COVID-19, requiring a multi-sectorial strategic approach and significant state-level efforts in coordinating federal, private sector, and donor assistance.

The federal government should adopt a strategic approach with international development partners, given that donor resources would also decline. This is the time when donor coordination will have greater utility. The federal government, through the Ministry of National Planning, should produce a plan for the health sector across the states or regions that donors can tap into. Donors want to be coordinated. But they want to be coordinated intelligently, purposefully, and transparently. This is an opportunity to reengineer Nigeria's donor relationships as well as to guide and focus their contribution. It would make sense if the highest level of government will lead this.

One critical area that Nigeria should exploit and invest in post-COVID-19 is pharmaceutical research and innovation. Pharmaceutical research centres and pharmacy faculties can be found in Nigerian universities. But, they lack research support. But more importantly, they don't get the stimuli that come from political leadership. Some of the COVID-19 resources should be directed to some selected institutions and coordinated to work collaboratively towards producing drugs that could address COVID-19 and other diseases that are prevalent in our society. Our dependence on foreign importation of drugs limits access and cannot be sustained over the long run. There are many drugs produced from our herbs on the market with NAFDAC numbers, but with a disclaimer that the efficacy of these drugs has not been verified. This is the time to equip NAFDAC and the universities to begin to verify and authenticate the safety and efficacy of these drugs. This is a worthwhile investment that would go a long way in breaking down self-doubt and knowledge dependence.

ii. Economy

Here are some of the challenges Nigeria has to contend with:

(1) Pronounced economic nationalism around the globe—my nation and my people first.
(2) Absence of Sympathy Credit: This is a pandemic, not a national or regional epidemic
(3) Significant reduction in foreign direct investment (especially in Nigeria's oil and gas sector)
(4) Significant reduction in immigrant remittances (now at over $15 billion per annum) due to unemployment. This could worsen Nigeria's poverty profile, especially in the South.
(5) Both demand and supply shocks. Demand shocks will reduce domestic and foreign consumption. The supply shock will affect Nigeria's supply chain, especially that of critical imports from China and other sources – especially capital goods and raw materials.
(6) No growth or recession

The countries that would rebound and prosper post COVID-19 are countries that are creating and producing things. We are describing a transforming economy; an innovation economy. The dominance of the service sector in our economy weakens the resilience of the Nigerian economy. It has made Nigeria import-dependent, with a huge wholesale and retail sector that contributes significantly to this import dependence. We must shift the significant middle class's spending from foreign-made goods to locally produced goods. But we must produce the goods at home first. Two sectors are critical in this respect: agriculture and manufacturing.

Agriculture

There have been some significant steps taken with respect to the transformation of the agricultural sector and reducing food imports. But to transform agriculture we must raise agricultural productivity significantly. That has not happened. It would not happen because Nigeria's agricultural policy has not recognised nor invested in the knowledge and technology required to raise productivity in agriculture. The Universities of Agriculture are not seen as centres of solutions and the Agricultural Research Institutes play very little role in the agricultural policy landscape. Nigeria needs to alter the current knowledge generation and knowledge transfer infrastructure in the agricultural sector. But science-led agriculture would require specialization, scaling-up, and commercialisation, treating agriculture as business. Currently, over 70 per cent of Nigeria's cultivated land is in the form of small holdings with less than 2 hectares per farmer. This is a major constraint with respect to the scaling-up of technological adoption. But both technology supply and demand face significant non-technological constraints that affect access and profitability. The resolution of these constraints would require the intervention of an intelligent and capable government. In order to take agriculture to the next level and produce at an internationally competitive level, the following should happen:

- Organise knowledge-generating and knowledge-transfer institutions regionally around the key crops of the regions.

- Scale-up and commercialise agriculture by providing incentives and inviting both local and international businessmen and women to participate (key crops can be identified).
- States and regions should have an agricultural rejuvenation plan with appropriate incentives.
- The federal and state governments should bring back the marketing boards. These boards constructed under the PPP must be by the private sector led. The traditional roles of the board—quality control, knowledge transfer, price stability, etc.—are critical now.
- Investment in post-harvest technology and the use of already constructed cold-storage facilities across the country should become a policy priority. Again, the private sector can become active players here].
- There should be a major plan to link agriculture more aggressively with manufacturing.

Manufacturing

To build resilience and address unemployment and poverty, Nigeria must take advantage of a post COVID-19 economy to increase the manufacturing sector's contribution to GDP from about 10 percent to 30 to 40 per cent. No country has ever taken millions out of poverty without a robust manufacturing sector. The technological dynamism in the sector raises productivity, raises wages and income, and hence leads to poverty reduction. But there cannot be a robust manufacturing sector that is innovative without active government support and intermediation. I would like to suggest the following:

- The Ministry of Industry must be on par with the Ministry of Agriculture in terms of budget allocation and status. Some of the budget allocation would come in handy for the resolution of first-mover disadvantages, for bridging infrastructural gaps, and for the aggressive acquisition of "settled" technology – mostly those in the public domain that require licensing, etc.
- Coordination failure is a major issue: -Given limited resources, institutions such as the Bank of Industry, NEXIM Bank, Bank of Agriculture, NEPC, and Raw Material Research and Development Council must bring their assets and resources to

promote selected key import substitution products. They should not be allowed to operate on a business-as-usual basis. The Central Bank of Nigeria would be required to invest its surplus in the manufacturing plan of the federal government.

- The export processing zones need to be reactivated and made to play a pivotal role in boosting the manufacturing sector. They can serve as enclaves and islands of infrastructure sufficiency for the production of goods with huge domestic demand and export potential. Their leadership must be appropriate and accountable.

- Nigeria can take advantage of the supply disruption in China and encourage Chinese investors to invest here with a programme of incentives. But these investments must be on agreed-upon terms that include strict enforcement of technology transfer, skills-upgrading, and domestic job creation with timelines. The idea is that Nigeria must move from "made in Nigeria" to "made-by Nigerians" over a specified period. This can only happen with a disciplined, committed, and capable government. This should be the government's attitude towards any other foreign investor interested in boosting the manufacturing sector.

- The government must work with the private sector and state governments to invest in technical and vocational skills, and in some instances, industry-specific skills. This is where the polytechnics and engineering schools can become useful in training skilled factory hands.

- Post COVID-19, the National Economic Council must be a council for how to generate jobs, raise productivity, and create wealth and prosperity. States must be seen as centres of prosperity, with plans on how to transform the many natural resources of the states into manufactured goods. States can act alone, but they can also present regional plans that the Federal government can incentivise.

- Some of our high-net worth individuals should be encouraged to shift some of their resources from the service sector to the manufacturing, sector with the federal government as the major partner and broker.

- The government must maintain policy consistency and use smart subsidies such as insurance and guarantees to promote manufacturing, provided it is not done in a reckless manner.

3
Talking Points on Infrastructure Financing In Nigeria

For a country mired in poverty, productivity growth and the overall growth of the economy are imperatives. If millions are going to be lifted out of poverty, the nation must produce (manufacture) and create jobs—but more importantly, it must produce competitively. And we must be concerned with both short- and long-term growth, hence the critical importance of investments in infrastructure that would drive productivity growth, raise income, and reduce poverty. Infrastructure is therefore the enabler that encourages both domestic and foreign direct investment and defines, in part, our competitive environment.

At our level of development, every investment in infrastructure would be growth-enhancing. But how do you prioritise among the wide array of amenities that are classified as infrastructure: electricity, roads and bridges, water supply and distribution systems, communication and digital connectivity, waste water collection and treatment facilities, waterways, sea ports, airports and airways facilities, mass transit facilities, railways, schools and health buildings, and solid-waste disposal facilities.

As may be evident, some of this infrastructure may be parceled out to semi-monopolies to provide and manage, with the government acting as a regulator. This could be case with electricity, communication, school, and health infrastructure. But most of the other infrastructure, especially in a developing country, will fall under the category of public infrastructure, – implying that it was publicly created, managed, and regulated. Another issue for discussion is whether governments can create and regulate but devolve management to the private sector, and what the pros and cons are? Particularly, in terms of access and the risks of inequality that may result from differential access.

Even with the advent of advanced technology that has made certain infrastructure divisible and therefore subject to market forces and profitable for private investors, underdevelopment makes it imperative that government remains the major provider for a couple of reasons. First, underdevelopment implies low income and inadequate demand for commercially priced infrastructure. Second, the huge initial outlay for most infrastructures limits the participation of the private sector. The third is consumer and employment protection. Fourth, there is a legitimate concern about income distribution and inequality. Other more theoretical reasons (and I don't want us to dismiss them) are issues around positive externalities, market failure, and free-rider problems that constrain private investor participation.

But some of these issues are now being dealt with by institutions of government that regulate and complement the activities of the private sector; by redefining the public good to allow for some restrictions in access, congestion pricing, tolling, and other forms of pay as use; and through public-private-partnerships (PPP); concessions; and privatisation with government equity.

After all is said and done, for a developing country like Nigeria, the provision of critical infrastructure is at the centre of the governance and development challenge. It is said that Nigeria requires 10 trillion Naira over ten years to bridge the infrastructure gap. You cannot rely on public provision alone because public revenue and tax revenue are very low because of the huge population living in poverty and the high unemployment and underemployment rate. The current trend of simply borrowing and investing in infrastructure is not sustainable because the revenue to service the debt is simply not there and there are competing demands from other sectors for public resources. In fact, a debt sustainability plan must be an integral part of a comprehensive infrastructure development plan, underscoring the many sources of financing, duration, and payback mechanisms. Nigeria comes up short in this regard. This is because infrastructure is treated more as a political tool than an economic enabler. A philosophy that needs to change. And then there is the additional issue of inefficiency and corruption in public infrastructure spending, inadequate capacity to create and manage infrastructure, poor budgetary management, and multi-year allocations that do not make sense. Then there is the issue of lack of coordination between the national and sub-national governments in infrastructure development and financing.

But what of private finance? The issue with private finance is that it is more discerning. There is a huge international private financing industry looking for profitable investments, and many emerging markets are tapping into it. Many countries, including Egypt,

Indonesia, Malaysia, and some countries in East Africa, are striving to update and review their PPP laws and institutional frameworks in an effort to open up their infrastructure sector to more private investment and finance. But there are institutional requirements to mitigate risks— a certain precondition and you can judge where Nigeria stands on these:

    a.   Security
    b.   Rule of law and certainty of contracts
    c.   Debt sustainability profile
    d.   Subsidy regimes that undermine market and investor confidence
    e.   Macroeconomic stability: exchange rate fluctuation, inflation
    f.   Political volatility and social unrest
    g.   Peculiar issues for Nigeria revolve around insecurity: terrorism, kidnapping, and banditry.

These issues are important because infrastructure projects are long-term, requiring a long gestation period and years of a stable revenue stream for payback and assurance of capital repatriation. This is why most proposals for a foreign capital investment in Nigeria's infrastructure ask for sovereign or international bank guarantee, invariably imposing additional costs on the projects. We can safely say that private international non-donor financing, is a limited option because of the issues raised above. We know that exchange rate fluctuations have hurt private capital that came into Nigeria to finance capital projects. But there are regulatory flexibilities and risk guarantees that can be deployed to cushion the effects of these issues.

We are left with local capital markets. The Nigerian capital market can be a source of financing for infrastructure. But even with this source, investors worry about long-term investment if inflation is not tamed. Pension funds and government bonds are in effect long-term savings that can be transformed into investment funds for infrastructure. If pension funds have N2 trillion in assets, a 10 per cent allocation of this fund (N200billion) for infrastructure investment can serve as a stimulant capital for infrastructure fund, acting as equity investment. Additional funds equivalent to two to three times this original amount can be raised as long-term debt capital in counterpart funding provided there are appropriate incentives. This is where domestic high-net-worth individuals become important. Guarantees may become necessary here as well. But the high cost of issuing corporate bonds must also be looked into.

What will the demand for infrastructure look like in the future based on consumer behaviour? How would technology affect the nature and use of infrastructure and what should be the macro response of governments?

There are now impact investors concerned about sustainability issues, and climate change, and the like. The market for impact investing is estimated to be worth around USD 500 billion. USD 500 billion is invested in green bonds.

Technology is creating new economic models, and infrastructure planning and investment must recognise these and become more consumer-centric. For instance, how would the falling prices of solar kits affect investment in power-generating assets in the future? How quickly would the demand for traditional energy sources drop? Who will serve as a residual supplier? Should there be new investments using public funds for new centralised energy grids? Evaluate how IPPs are currently shaping energy demand and supply in a place like Lagos? Should it be encouraged nationwide?

CHAPTER THIRTEEN

Preparing Nigeria's Socio-Political and Economic Environment for the Fourth Industrial Revolution

When national institutions are concerned with issues of now, it is very refreshing to find national institutions seeking answers, asking questions around an imminent disruptive technology that would shape the productive landscape of the world, and; being contemplative about a set of technologies that would alter the nature of work. And the central question would revolve around how prepared Nigeria is to take advantage of these technologies and to minimise the negative effects. In other words, what are the signposts that Nigeria should put in place as a participant in a global technology space as she awaits the fourth industrial revolution.

It must be noted that while the fourth industrial revolution is around the corner – in fact, some elements of it are already with us— one cannot lose sight of the fact that Nigeria and most of Africa are still grappling with issues of the second industrial revolution that seemingly ended in 1914. We are still unable to feed Nigeria (Africa). Our access to electricity is poor. We are still celebrating the completion of a few kilometres of railroad track. The standard of hygiene and sanitation is the lowest of all regions of the world. Our manufacturing sector, contributing less than 8 percent of GDP—one of the lowest in the world—have not made use of existing advanced technology. In addition, we are still grappling with low school enrollment and very low research output from our institutions. All these issues were resolved by the second industrial revolution and should be assumed. I was invited by the African Development Bank in 2019 to discuss the fourth industrial revolution in Abidjan. I reminded the audience that the Africa Development Bank (AfDB), by its organising framework, the High 5s, was focusing primarily on second industrial revolution concerns: light up and power Africa, feed Africa, industrialise Africa, integrate Africa, and improve the quality of life for the people of Africa. It is, therefore, difficult to mobilise citizens to meaningfully engage in the fourth industrial revolution without settling these issues.

But the issues of now and those of the future are not mutually exclusive. The path to the resolutions of issues now requires creative thinking and the concerted effort of an intelligent government that galvanises the generation and use of cutting-edge technology that forms the launch pad for the fourth industrial revolution. If we fail to act, like most global issues, Nigeria and Africa will be compelled to undergo a forced transition. Inevitably, the few who have the ability to embrace these technologies will reap the benefits, further widening the societal inequality. This widening gap has serious consequences for the socio-political and economic stability of the country. Bridging this gap is an issue every responsive government must address.

The characterisation of the fourth industrial revolution leads one to clearly articulate the uses and potential uses of these technologies, especially big data. Computers will be able to analyse millions of pieces of data in seconds, allowing institutions (businesses) to draw conclusions and make predictions about all aspects of our lives. I wonder, as an economist, if our major analytical role would not be taken over by machines able to manipulate big data and derive policy options more accurately. The scramble for these data is already on. This must not only be emphasised, but also the dangers inherent in the application of this technology, such as invasion of privacy and breach of national security. But we must also note that these big data can be deployed for good in business innovation and national planning.

Let me emphasise that, as one who was once in charge of our national planning, accurate data is at the soul of national planning. But machines and the speed of computation are one thing, and developing the processes of collecting the data and changing the mental mode of the political leadership and citizens towards accurate data are another. This is where we have a lot of work to do. States and local governments do not show significant interest in planning or data gathering. Citizens are not sensitised on the importance of data and their accuracy. Accurate data is empowering and can become a powerful instrument for international negotiations. The research, planning and statistics units of most government institutions in Nigeria do not perform the functions assigned to them but have become the focal point for contract tendering boards. The ease with which we falsify and manipulate data in this country to gain certain advantages is disturbing. Why are people born twenty or ten years ago still using affidavits to declare their age? Technology can only do what you ask it to do. The human element is critical to the efficacy of any technology. If we must take advantage of the fourth industrial revolution and big data, we need a reorientation at all levels, attitudinal change, a revolution in data gathering, and investment in establishing robust accompanying processes.

As I I previously stated, there are potential risks associated with technology, such as private and national security breaches, as we have seen in election interference in advanced democracies. These dangers are real. For a country like Nigeria, grappling with many issues, it would be easy not to pay attention to these dangers. There is a critical need for consumer protection and data protection with respect to national security. Importantly, there is also the need for an accompanying, robust regulatory framework that provides incentives for data protection and sanctions for infringement of privacy.

I need to elaborate on another important point—the issue of promoting inter-agency cooperation. Science, Technology, and Innovation, and for that matter, issues concerning the fourth industrial revolution require a cooperative attitude across many agencies: the Ministry of Science and Technology (as a coordinating ministry), the Ministry of Industry, the Ministry of Communication and Digital Economy, the Ministry of Education, the Ministry of National Planning, the Ministry of Finance, the Ministry of Agriculture, the Ministry of Defense, the Presidency, and the National Assembly. The critical problem Nigeria faces with respect to policy formulation and implementation is associated with coordination failure. Ministries act as silos with overlapping responsibilities that lack harmonisation. There is territoriality, with ministers and bureaucrats concerned with protecting and expanding their turf without due patriotic attention to the big picture or the over-arching goals. There are several parastatals that are misaligned in terms of their supervisory ministry, with objectives that are now observed in breach. The low productivity and accountability of many of these agencies weaken their position as frontline agencies for addressing the issues of the fourth industrial revolution. In terms of coordination, the Presidency must be very clear with respect to policy direction and the enforcement of a cooperative attitude among relevant agencies. The agencies must be manned and administered by competent hands that have the capacity to deliver on the mandates.

The National Assembly should set up a Committee of the Future with a special mandate for examining Nigeria's requirements for effective appropriation of new technologies. It should exercise its appropriation powers by insisting on budgetary provisions for science technology and innovation of the future and provide incentives for inter-agency collaboration.

The Intersection of Science, Technology, and Innovation and Poverty Reduction

Economic growth is fundamental to poverty reduction. For any significant reduction in the population of the poor in any country, the economy does not just grow but must grow consistently over a long period of time. But we have also witnessed economic growth in Nigeria, albeit for a short duration and without a concomitant reduction in poverty. In fact poverty was rising at the same time when our economy was growing by about 6-7 per cent per annum for about six year between 2005 and 2011, calling into question the argument for a growth-only model for poverty reduction. The argument for a growth-centered model is clear, as the leading proponent, distinguished Prof. Jagdish Bhagwati stated: "growth would pull the poor into gainful employment, thereby helping to lift them out of poverty... and that higher income will help them to increase their personal spending on health and education". In a paper I published while at the Brookings Institution in Washington DC as a visiting scholar, Towards Inclusive Growth in Nigeria, I provided a counter-narrative for the case of Nigeria. I made the following points:

> Growth is a necessary but not sufficient condition for poverty reduction. Of critical importance is the source of economic growth. At that time, rising oil prices were a major driver of our expansion. Because the petrochemical value chain with a higher value added has not been developed, the oil industry in Nigeria has low employment across the economy. The agricultural sector, which contributed about 50 per cent of the non-oil Gross Domestic Product at that time, has not raised the incomes and assets of the poor because it is still largely subsistence, low-tech, low productivity, and lacking in specialisation, scale-up, and commercialisation.

As net purchasers of food, inflation ate deep into the income of the farmer, preventing them from spending on their health and the education of their children. The service sector, a strong contributor to the GDP, has a narrow wage employment base. I made two additional important points: that the absence of a robust manufacturing sector was the singular most important factor in explaining the absence of inclusive growth.

No country has successfully lifted millions out of poverty without a large manufacturing sector. It is the sector with the most significant technological spillover linkages with other sectors of the economy, a huge wage employment base, and higher incomes from higher productivity. It is also the sector where industrial and technological upgrading occurs, which is key to structural change, sustained economic growth, and hence poverty reduction. In essence, when economic growth is from a growing manufacturing sector, that growth is likely to be inclusive and reduce poverty, especially if it is characterised by huge labour demand. Unfortunately, our economy has not diversified into manufacturing; its contribution to GDP is still about 12 per cent, compared to that of emerging economies, which is between 20 and 30 percent with rising productivity. Nigeria's performance is largely due to government's misunderstanding of its role in assisting incipient entrepreneurs in overcoming the cost of infrastructural deficits and risks associated with "first mover disadvantages" according to Justin Lin, a former Chief Economist at the World Bank. Added to this is the problem with our Federalism, where states do not serve as "engines of national prosperity" or "centres for policy and economic innovation" and are not held accountable for the poverty or unemployment rates in their states.[99]

From the foregoing, it is clear that I am a proponent of manufacturing-sector induced economic growth. Sustained economic growth, irrespective of the source, is driven by a consistent increase in productivity. And productivity is largely driven by technology and innovation. If any nation wants to reduce the population of its citizens who are poor, it must invest in or create policies that encourage the use of technology to increase the productivity of its citizens. It is increased productivity that raises the income and assets of the poor. Agriculture and manufacturing are two critical sectors in Nigeria where technology-induced growth would help lift many people out of poverty. The important question before us is whether the emerging technology and innovation under the fourth industrial revolution would, given our socio-economic and political contexts, enhance or diminish the productivity of the poor. And how may the nation prepare to take advantage of this innovative force in the face of our poor human capital—low skill, low-wage workforce?

The Fourth Industrial Revolution and the Future of Work

Throughout history, there have been three industrial revolutions corresponding to major technological discoveries and innovations that transformed economic processes and improved the productivity of the workers and their standard of living. The first revolution (1750-1850) witnessed the mechanisation of industry, mechanisation of factories, systems, specialisation, and division of labour, the development of machine tools, the extraction of coal, the steam engine, and the manufacturing of railroads etc. The second (1850–1914) was marked by the discovery and use of electricity, gas, oil, telegraph, and telephone. The third revolution, the digitisation revolution in the late 1900s, was marked by the spread of computers and electronics, the invention of the internet, biotechnology, nuclear power, the automation of entire production processes, etc., the technology of the first and second industrial revolutions was biased towards lower-skilled workers. They brought millions of unskilled workers into factories but put skilled artisans such as blacksmiths and hand weavers out of work. This was the beginning of prosperity in Britain and parts of Europe and America. However, both the third and the fourth industrial revolutions "embodied skill-based technological change"[100]. This bias is further accentuated in the fourth industrial revolution as work becomes intensively intelligence-driven rather than labour-driven and the governance and practices of the workplace change dramatically. We are already witnessing some of this.

If you examine the first and second industrial revolutions that seemingly ended in 1914, you would realise that Nigeria is still grappling with key elements—we are still trying to light Nigeria, feed Nigeria, and industrialise Nigeria. Nigerians celebrate when a few kilometres of rail are laid. As stated earlier, our manufacturing is at best very low-tech, as we pay lip service to industrial diversification and treat it casually as a "natural phenomenon". And now the fourth industrial revolution is upon us, and we are likely to undergo another forced transition because of the state of our unpreparedness. However, we must acknowledge the significant progress we have made in catching up with telecommunication technology, especially in the banking sector. But this catch-up, like in most technologies, represents only our capacity to use another people's technology but not our ability to produce or reproduce it—an important point to note in our transformation journey. And this is where the China model—the deployment of what I have called "settled technology", the use and adaptation of technology that is in the public or semi-public domain to increase their productivity and economic growth—provides important lessons for shared prosperity. In 1990, the rate of poverty in China was 66.6 per cent, and today it is less than 2 percent[101]. And note that, in the words of these authors, "alleviating poverty is not the same as creating prosperity". This is an important distinction for policy construction.

In order to prepare Nigeria for the fourth industrial revolution, you must appreciate the future of work and the skills required to be an active participant in the labour market of tomorrow. As we already know, there are four main technologies driving the Fourth Industrial Revolution: Artificial Intelligence, Machine Learning, Internet of Things (IoT), and Big Data. Space technology is another one, but it is mostly going to be affected by advances in the other four. The jobs of the future will mainly revolve around these technologies - jobs dealing with their development, management, and application. These would require highly specialised skills.

These technologies have the potential to transform every aspect of our lives. They have applications in agriculture, security, education, medicine, services, mobility, governance, the arts, etc. The impact they could have on our lives has been described as limitless. These technologies can potentially increase productivity growth across many sectors. One of the downsides of the advances in these technologies is that they have the potential to render many current jobs obsolete. The need for human workers in certain industries will be reduced as it becomes more costly and less efficient to employ actual people in certain roles. Drivers will become obsolete with the adoption of autonomous vehicles, manufacturing and agriculture will require less human labour as automation and robotics become more advanced, and big data and machine learning have the potential to disrupt healthcare, journalism, and insurance, removing the need for many professionals in those industries. The list goes on. With high unemployment, underemployment, fragile employment, huge informal sector employment, and many working poor, Nigeria must be concerned about this disruptive technology and its implications for its structural transformation goals, especially manufacturing sector-led industrialization. However, the Fourth Industrial Revolution will come with a host of new industries and jobs, not just jobs in relation to the technologies mentioned above, but also jobs in creative and problem-solving industries, in precision agriculture, in deepening services in mobile banking, in 3-D printing that can facilitate the construction of specialised equipment that is associated with the extractive industry, and in the delivery of education and health services.

Along with the changes in specific jobs will come a change in what the workplace looks like. Increased video and cross-collaboration technology will reduce the need for traditional office space and "9-5" roles. The current COVID-19 pandemic has demonstrated the possibilities around virtual meeting, conferences, and e-learning. I must say that the telecommunications sector in Nigeria did not disappoint, except that coverage is not uniform across the nation and access is still limited by cost. In the future, more workers will telecommute, and coming into the office will no longer be a requirement for many offices. This will increase the number of opportunities for seasonal and freelance work, as well as open up employers to a larger pool of potential employees who would be able to work from anywhere in the world. But this will require not only new skills, a new mindset, re-orientation, and discipline but also changes in Nigeria's labour laws.

Specific impacts on the poor: Artificial Intelligence (AI) can be used to map where they are, their access to water and other social and welfare-enhancing resources. It will reduce the cost of housing surveys. It can be used in agriculture to improve soil quality, detect crop diseases, predict crop yields, control pests, and eventually use robots for harvesting, among other thing. In the future, it will become an important tool for the management of disasters and for directing relief to the needy more appropriately. In education, technology can improve access to education for the poor through distance learning where space is not a constraint as well as by identifying and meeting the learning needs of children from poor parental background. The technology can also be a source of financial inclusion for the poor.

What skills do we need to build in Nigeria and Africa?

There are many things that are needed in order for Africa to catch up to the rest of the world and not lag further behind in terms of growth and human development. The current African labour force is mostly characterised by large informal and agricultural sectors that are often low in productivity and wages. The Fourth Industrial Revolution will make the low-skill, broad-based manufacturing employment path to prosperity a less viable option, at least in the long term. According to a World Economic Forum (WEF)[102] report on the future of Jobs in Africa, it is projected that an average of 46 per cent of the jobs in Ethiopia, Kenya, South Africa, and Nigeria are susceptible to automation. This number is likely to increase as the costs associated with automation fall. The same WEF report states that the current workforce is already inadequately skilled for the current jobs, according to employers who state this reason as a major business constraint.

The jobs of the future are highly skill-intensive and require specific expertise. They would revolve mainly around the main technologies of the Fourth Industrial Revolution. Workers in Africa need to be enabled to take advantage of these technologies and not be rendered obsolete by them. Along with the skills and technology required to have modern education, health, and green industries; the skills Africa would need to build are in Science, Technology, Engineering and Mathematics (STEM), skills in automation, logistics, IoT, and robotics to increase agricultural output as well as transition to high tech manufacturing and agricultural sectors, skills in information and computer technology (ICT) to transition to a modern service sector. Skills are needed for future infrastructure design and development as well as green technologies for energy and its related industries. Creative skills for modern creative industries are something else that will be critical for Africa but are not discussed as much as the more technical skills. Professions in art, music, design, literature, and film will need skilled professionals. These new industries will be affected by the technologies mentioned earlier, but more so in a collaborative sense. Skilled human innovation combined with these technologies will enhance and improve the output of these creative industries as well as serve to improve the technical industries as well.

How Do We Build These Skills?

Most of the strategies revolving around mitigating the effects of the fourth IR involve "worker retraining" and updating the skills of workers to reflect the needs of the current and future job landscape. The strategy for Nigeria and Africa has to be a little different. The labour force is currently made up of mostly low-skilled workers with low levels of productivity. Education systems across Africa are archaic and severely underfunded. Universities are not regarded, as in Israel and other advanced countries, as centres of solutions with significant R&D and innovation roles. According to a UNDP report, only one in six African college students (17 per cent) will graduate with a Science, Technology, Engineering, or Mathematics (STEM) degree - meaning most of the recent graduates are not well placed to take advantage of the jobs and technologies of the future. Nigeria has no single world-class engineering laboratory in any university. The curriculum is outdated, and there is no inbuilt relevant practical training that connects theory to practice. Policymakers seeking foreign investments must understand that "made in Nigeria" does not mean "made by Nigerians". As we build the railways, will we be able to maintain or reproduce them many years from now? The WEF report indicates that human capital optimisation - education, skills development and deployment throughout the life-course- in Nigeria is 49 percent when the global average is 65, and Mauritius (65), Ghana (64) and South Africa (63).

There has to be a concerted effort to ensure that new entrants into the labor force are equipped with the skills needed to take part in the labor market of the future. The WEF report puts it very succinctly: "To build a pipeline of future skills, Africa's educators should design future-ready curricula that encourage critical thinking, creativity, and emotional intelligence as well as accelerate the acquisition of digital and STEM skills to match the way people will work and collaborate in the

Fourth Industrial Revolution". In addition to this, governments should instill a culture that encourages continuous learning. Governments and businesses would also need to work together to come up with innovative ways to address the skills gap. There are programmes such as the Lambda School, which offers intensive skills acquisition learning in Web development, data science, et al. for no upfront cost - with payments only made after employment with wages over USD 50,000. They recently started a partnership with a Nigerian payments platform, PayStack, for an employment pipeline. Purdue University in the US has started a similar programme for its students: an Income Share Agreement. Preparing Nigeria for the fourth industrial revolution will require re-thinking our entire educational system with clear roles for governments at all levels and the private sector. It requires a budgetary provision that signals an acknowledgement of the significance of the sector in our socio-economic and political development. Incentives should be provided to encourage students to enroll in STEM degrees and to pursue advanced and research degrees in these areas.

The Fourth Industrial Revolution and Nigeria's Innovation Gap

For both developed and developing countries, one of the ways to replace lost jobs and generate growth remains through innovation, and much of that innovation will come from start-ups. It is difficult to find a developed or emerging economy that does not want more start-ups and greater entrepreneurship[103]. [The Chinese government, not to mention the hundreds of thousands of new engineers graduating in China each year, is determined to shift from "Made in China" to "Made by China". In the next few years, we may see China leapfrog America in the leadership of whole industries, such as the development and manufacture of electric cars and the batteries that power them. India is also becoming a science and technology powerhouse.][104]

It has become clear that nations that have transformed, where structural change has occurred, growth has been sustained, gainful employment and incomes have risen, shared prosperity has been generated, and millions have been lifted out of poverty, are innovation economies. Economies that produce things and have command of the means of producing goods and services. They are nations that are not content with things being produced in their country but can reproduce the goods themselves. To attain this status requires significant investment in the innovation infrastructure of the country, both physical and human. So, what is the state of Nigeria's innovation trajectory?

To understand our state of preparedness for the fourth industrial revolution, I decided to examine Nigeria's ranking on the Global Innovation Index, an annual ranking of nations according to their innovation capabilities. According to the authors of GII, "it aims to capture the multi-dimensional facets of innovation using about 80 indicators". It ranks 131 countries around the world. In 2020, Nigeria ranked 117; in 2019, 114; and in 2018, 118. In terms of its innovation output, it is ranked 121 in 2020, a rank lower than 105 in 2019 and 115 in 2018. Nigeria ranks 25th among the 29 lower middle-income group economies and 15th among the 26th economies in Sub-Saharan Africa. Overall, Nigeria has not made progress. The report notes that "relative to the gross domestic product (GDP), Nigeria's performance is below expectations for its level of development". And "Nigeria produces less innovation outputs relative to its level of innovation investments." Using the seven GII pillars, Nigeria performed below average in five pillars when compared to other sub-Saharan African countries. These are: institutions, human capital and research, infrastructure, knowledge and technology outputs, and creative outputs. Only in two pillars, market sophistication and business sophistication, was Nigeria above average. Further disaggregation of Nigeria's strengths and weaknesses revealed that our overall poor ranking came from a few key indicators. Nigeria ranked 129 on political environment, 128 on political and operational stability; 128 on creative goods exports as a percent of total trade, 125 on domestic credit to the private sector as a percent of GDP; and 122 on university-industry research collaboration. The weak university-industry research collaboration underscores the absence of a national system of innovation that not only identifies the players and assigns roles but accords significance to the interactions among the players; allowing the flexibility of knowledge flows among universities, research institutions, private sector enterprises, governments, and NGOs in supporting a knowledge economy.

From the Global Innovation Index indicators, one can clearly see that institutions that generate policies that govern science, technology, and innovation are critical in determining innovation outcomes. Some of these institutions exist in Nigeria. However, these institutions need to be reorganised and refocused—by streamlining their mandate, providing adequate funding, and having a performance-driven leadership with targets. If Nigeria is to close the innovation gap, the states, the federal government, and the private sector must work collaboratively. The National Economic Council (NEC) is a good starting point for fostering this collaboration. The NEC is a powerful institutional arrangement that can be used to provide incentives for states to work with the federal government on issues of the Fourth Industrial Revolution. It can also be used creatively to foster regional cooperation in science and technology as a critical step in establishing an effective national system of innovation. Such incentives can include directing federal government counterpart funding and donor assistance to states that meet certain S, T, and I parameters. establishment of a national science and technology fund is long overdue. The fund, properly set up and managed, can focus on closing the innovation gap and supporting the adaptation of "settled technology" for improved productivity across sectors. It will also fund cutting-edge research. Attempts were made in the past to set up the fund, but it never got off the ground because science and technology continue to be of low priority for successive governments. I have suggested in another presentation that the monies being recovered from corrupt officials can be used to create such a fund, turning a bad act into the creation of public goods. Finally, the military's research and development should rise to the level where the outcome of their efforts would feed the civilian industrial complex, as we have seen in Israel and elsewhere. The gaps in innovation, and hence our lack of readiness for the fourth industrial revolution, will continue to exist unless we address, in, a very significant way, STEM education from the primary school to the university and make significant investments in research and development. This is in addition to encouraging market-creating innovation, as we saw with the telecommunication industry in Nigeria.

Index

A

Aba, 117, 118, 119, 120, 121, 123, 124, 126, 127
Abia Think Thank Association, 118
Acemoglu, Daron, 35, 61, 64, 94, 195
Adams, John, 156
Africa Development Bank, 177
Africa Magic, 46
Ake, Claude, 53, 85
Allied forces, 21, 22
Arkansas Science and Development Authority, 125
Artificial Intelligence, 183, 184
Atlantic Magazine, 21
Awolowo, Obafemi, 70, 78, 79, 80
Ayogu, Melvin, 121
Azikiwe, Nnamdi, 78

B

Balewa, Abubakar Tafawa, 31
Banana Island, 70
Bernasek, Anna, 79
Bhagwati, Jagdish, 104, 180
bin Laden, Osama, 151
Boko Haram, 24, 149, 151
Bureau of Public Enterprise, 131

C

Catholic homily, 47
Central Bank of Nigeria, 158, 171
Chattered Institute of Personnel Management, 28
Christianity, 47
Ciroma, Adamu, 78
COVID-19., 165, 166
Culture and temperament, 21

D

Defence Intelligence Agency, 150
Democratic Republic of Congo, 35
Department of Homeland Security, 160
Development planning, 85, 100
Directorate of Airforce Intelligence, 150
Directorate of Military Intelligence, 150

Directorate of Naval Intelligence Agency, 150
Dompere, Koffi Kissi, 16
Douglas, Fredrick, 40, 54, 137, 148, 195

E

Economic and Financial Crimes Commission, 158
Economist Intelligence Unit, 109
Ehahoro, Anthony, 78
Emperor Hirohito, 21
Esele, Peter, 25
Ethiopia, 105, 185

F

Federal Inland Revenue Service, 158, 166
Federal Protective Services, 160
Fisher, Marx, 21
Fourth Industrial Revolution, 182, 183, 184, 185, 186, 187, 189
Frankel, Victor E., 44, 142

G

Gandhi, Mahatma, 28, 41, 140, 148
Global Innovation Index, 188
Globalisation, xi, 16, 130
Goldwater, Barry, 161
Greene, Joshua, 77
Guangzhou, 65, 96, 113, 122

H

Harrison, Lawrence, 29, 195
Hiroshima, 22
Howard University, xi, 16, 17
Huntington, Samuel, 29, 195
Hussein, Saddam, 156

I

Immigration and Naturalisation Service, 160
Independent Corrupt Practices and Other Related Offences Commission, 158
India, 98, 105, 108, 109, 187
Indian Planning Commission, 109
Innoson Motors, 113

References and endnotes

1 Richard, G.W and Kate, Pickett. (2010). The Spirit Level; Why Greater Equality Makes Society Stronger (Harlow, England: Penguin Books

2 Richard, G.W and Kate, Pickett. (2010). The Spirit Level; Why Greater Equality Makes Society Stronger (Harlow, England: Penguin Books)

3 The Emperor's Speech: Hirohito Transformed Japan Forever, Coursehero.com/file/10351694, accessed February 9, 2023.

4 Hebert, P. Bix. (2000). Hirohito and the Making of Modern Japan (New York, Harper Collins Publisher)

5 Hirohito Surrender Broadcast, Wikipedia, Accessed February 8, 2023.

6 The White House 2009, *President Barack Obama's Inaugural Address*, United State of America Government, Accessed February 15, 2018 https://obamawhitehouse.arch ives.gov/blog/2009/01/21/president-Barack-obamas-inaugural-address

7 Harrison, L.E. and Huntington, S.P.(2000). Culture Matters; *How Values Shape Human Progress* (New York, NY:Basic Books).

8 Lee, Kuan Yew (2000). From Third World to first: The Singapore Story;1965 – 2000, (New York: Harper Collins Publishers)

9 Gorge, F.G (1985). The Spirit of Enterprise, (New York: Simon & Schuster Publisher)

10 Acemoglu, Daron and James, Robinson (2013). Why Nations Fail: The Origins of power, prosperity, and power, (New York: Pbk. Ed. Crown Business)

11 Sachs, Jeffrey (2011). The Price of Civilization: Economics and Ethics After the Fall, (London: Bodley Head, Random House). pp.160-183.

12 Stanford Center on Poverty and Inequality,2020, *Fredrick Douglas Quotes*, Stanford University, Accessed January 28, 2020
https://inequality.stanford.edu/publications/quote/frederick-douglass

13 Sidney, Poitier (2008). Life Beyond Measure: Letters to My Great-granddaughter, (New York: Simon & Schuster Publisher)

14 Viktor, E.Frankl (1962). Man's Search for meaning: An introduction to logotherapy, (Boston:Beacon Press)

15 Lee, Kuan Yew (2000). From Third World to first: The Singapore Story;1965 – 2000, (New York: Harper Collins Publishers)

16 Sen, Amartya. (2006). Identity and Violence: The illusion of destiny, (New York: W.W. Norton & Co.)

17 Annual Lecture of the Chartered Institute of Bankers of Nigeria, delivered on June 15, 2017, Bankers House, Victoria Island, Lagos. Full citation for the references in this lecture would be provided later.

18 Sen Amartya. New York: Anchor Books; London: Allen & Unwin; 1999. 1928. Freedom as Development; p. p. 242. as cited from Rabindranath Tagore, Letters to a Friend.

19 North, D.C. (1999). Understanding the process of economic change, (London: Institute of Economic Affairs)

20 This section benefitted from my in-depth discussions with Dr. Ben Nwosu, a political science scholar at the Institute for Development Studies, University of Nigeria, Enugu Campus.

[21] Duverger, M. (1964). Political Parties: Their Organization and Activity in the modern State. London: Methuen

[22] Ake, Claude. (1967). A Theory of Political Integration. Homewood, Illinois: Dorsey Press.

[23] Rawls, John, 1921-2002 author. (1971). A theory of Justice, Cambridge, Massachusetts: The Belknap Press of Harvard University Press.

[24] Richard, G.W. and Kate Pickett (2010). Op. cit.

[25] In Nigeria, not even the Peoples Democratic Party (PDP) could maintain policy consistency in its 16 year rule. The refineries were sold by the Obasanjo's regime and reversed by the Yar'Dua's government that took over and this is just one example.

[26] Mohamad, Mahathir (2012). Doctor in the House: The Memoirs of Tun Dr. Mahathir Mohamad, (Published by MPH group publishing Sdn Bhd, Selangor Malaysia).

[27] Mohamad, Mahathir (2012). Doctor in the House: The Memoirs of Tun Dr. Mahathir Mohamad, (Published by MPH group publishing Sdn Bhd, Selangor Malaysia).

[28] Lin, Ling and Liu, Shi-Qing, "New Growth Poles for Chinese Economy: Discussion on Certain Issues in Building the Chengdu-Chongqing Growth Pole", Sichuan Academy of Social Sciences, Sichuan, Chengdu, 610072 (undated but accessed in the internet on 5/11/2015).

[29] KPMG China (2011). "China's Five-Year Plan: Overview", KPMG China, March, 2011

[30] WWW.\\homelessworldcup.org/homelessness-statistics (accessed on November 10, 2019).

[31] The American Presidency Project 1945, *Franklin D. Roosevelt State of the Union Address*, University of California, Accessed 21 September 2022 https://www.presidency.ucsb.edu/documents/state-the-union-address

[32] Ng Kok Hoe (). Public Housing Policy in Singapore, in global-is-asian.

[33] Green, J.D. (2013). Moral tribes: Emotion, Reason, and the Gap between Us and Them. (New York: The Penguin Press)

[34] Taken from my paper, Ogbu, Osita (2013). "Aba: A Potential Engine of Prosperity and the Infrastructural Imperatives",Invited Lecture Delivered at the Aba Summit On "Abia Development: Aba as a Centre of Entrepreneurial Excellence", On Wednesday, November 20, 2013 At The Hotel Terminus, Azikiwe Road, Aba.

[35] Yew, Lee Kuan (2000).From Third World to First, (Harper Collins Publishers) New York N. Y. USA

[36] Yew, Lee Kuan (2000).From Third World to First, (Harper Collins Publishers) New York N. Y. USA

[37] Bernasek, Anna. (2010). The Economics of Integrity, (New York: Harper Collins Publishers)

[38] Ake, Claude (1996). Democracy and Development in Africa, The Bookings Institution, Washington, D.C.

39 Ogbu, Osita (2008). "Intellectuals and Development", Adada Public Lecture, under the Auspices of the Association of Nsukka Professors.

40 Sen, Amartya (1999). Development as Freedom, First Anchor Books, N.Y., New York, USA.

41 This contradiction, the presence of schools and absence of learning, would lead to the more disturbing inequality of the future as poor families are left with no choice but to send their kids to poorly equipped public schools that would limit their capability and ability to take advantage of future economic opportunities.

42 Sach, Ignacy. (2004). Inclusive Development Strategy in an Era of Globalization, ILO Working Paper No. 35. PP. 10-11.

43 Ogbu, Osita. "Development as Attitude", Public Lecture delivered under the auspices of the Ezike Diamond Club, at the Grace Manor Hotel, October, 2011.

44 Sach, Ignacy. (2004). Inclusive Development Strategy in an Era of Globalization, ILO Working Paper No. 35.

45 This quotation and the preceding discussion benefited from Sen, Amartya (1999). Development As Freedom, Op. cit., pp. 274-278.

46 Ajakaiye, O. (2014). Development Planning in Mixed Economies: Morphology and Future Directions for Africa. Presidential Address, The Nigerian Economic Society, 55th Annual Conference, Abuja, Nigeria.
Ajakaiye, O. (2015). Development Planning in Contemporary Nigeria, Presidential Address, The Nigerian Economic Society, 56th Annual Conference, Abuja, Nigeria.

47 Ikeanyiuba, M. O. (2009). "Development Planning in Nigeria: Reflections on the NEEDS 2003-2007", Journal of Social Science, 20 (3), 197-210.

48 Yew, Lee Kuan (2000). From Third World to First, (Harper Collins Publishers) New York N. Y. USA

49 In Nigeria, not even the Peoples Democratic Party (PDP) could maintain policy consistency in its 16 year rule. The refineries were sold by the Obasanjo's regime and reversed by the Yar'Dua's government that took over and this is just one example.

50 Mohamad, Mahathir (2012). Doctor in the House: The Memoirs of Tun Dr. Mahathir Mohamad, (Published by MPH group publishing Sdn Bhd, Selangor Malaysia).

51 Lin, Ling and Liu, Shi-Qing, "New Growth Poles for Chinese Economy: Discussion on Certain Issues in Building the Chengdu-Chongqing Growth Pole", Sichuan Academy of Social Sciences, Sichuan, Chengdu, 610072 (undated but accessed in the internet on 5/11/2015).

52 KPMG China (2011). "China's Five-Year Plan: Overview", KPMG China, March, 2011

53 Ogbu, Osita (2010). "On the Global Finncial crisis, "Creative Destruction" and the "New Market Economy", in Eboh and Ogbu (eds.). The Global Economic Crisis and Nigeria: Taking the Right Lessons, Avoiding the Wrong Lessons, (African Institute for Applied Economics, Enugu, Nigeria).

[54] Sheng, Andrew. "If China, India and Malaysia want to meet their five-year plan goals, they must invest in their people", South China Morning Post, October 30, 2015.

[55] The Economist 11 December 2011, *Africa Rising,* The Economist Group, Accessed 12 December 2011 https://www.economist.com/leaders/2011/12/03/africa-rising

[56] Bhagwati, Jagdish. 2011. "Does Redistributing Income Reduce Poverty?" *Chazen Global Insights*, November 3, 2011.

[57] Data is for 2006 from the Development Data Group, The World Bank, 2008. Although dated, the data was used for illustration purposes.

[58] Rodrik, D. (2007). "Normalizing Industrial Policy". Cambridge, MA: John F. Kennedy School of Government, Harvard University. Mimeo.

[59] Rodrick, D. (2004). "Industrial Policy for the Twenty-First Century", Cambridge, MA: John F. Kennedy School of Government, Harvard University. Mimeo.

[60] IChemE Fellow and SembCorp Utilities VP, Jane Atkinson, shared her views on strategies for boosting UK manufacturing during a fringe meeting held at the Liberal Democrats' annual party conference in Liverpool, 27th September, 2010.

[61] Rana Foroohar, "Companies Are the New Countries", Time Magazine, February 13, 2013.

[62] Rodrik, D. (2007). "Normalizing Industrial Policy". Cambridge, MA: John F. Kennedy School of Government, Harvard University. Mimeo.

[63] Chang, Ha-Joon. Bad Samaritan: The Guilty Secrets of Rich Nations & the Threat to Global Prosperity, Random House Business Books, 2008.

[64] Homi Kharas, Koji Makino and Woojin Jung, Brookings Institution (full citation to be provided).

[65] Niranjan Rajadhyaksha, "India's New Industrial Policy", Café Economics, liveMint.com & World Street Journal, February 17, 2012.

[66] Fareed Zakaria "Like it or not (I don't), We Need Manufacturing Policy to Stay Competitive", Time Magazine, January 26, 2012

[67] This paper was written in 2012. The data is outdated but the lessons are important.

[68] John Litwack, Nigeria Economic Report, The World Bank, Abuja, July 22, 2014

[69] McKinsey Global Institute, McKinsey & Company (July, 2014). Nigeria's Renewal: Delivering Inclusive Growth in Africa's Largest Economy.

[70] This section is from the Policy Paper I did at Brookings Institution. Ogbu, Osita (2012). "Towards Inclusive Growth in Nigeria", Policy Paper 2012-3, Global Economy and Development, Brookings Institution

[71] Katz, Bruce. 2012. "Remaking Federalism to Remake the American Economy." Brookings Institution, Campaign 2012 Papers

[72] President Barack Obama, The State of the Union Address, January 2012.

[73] Invited Lecture Delivered at the Aba Summit on "Abia Development: Aba as a centre of entrepreneurial excellence", on Wednesday, November 20, 2013 at the Hotel Terminus, Azikiwe Road, Aba

[74] Simon Sinek (2009). Start With Why – How Great Leaders Inspire to take Action. (Brentford UK: Portfolio).

[75] Sachs, Jeffery. (2011). The Price of Civilization: Reawakening American Virtue and Prosperity. (New York: Random House)

[76] Rodrik, D. (2007). "Normalizing Industrial Policy". Cambridge, MA: John F. Kennedy School of Government, Harvard University. Mimeo.

[77] Presented at the inaugural conference of the Ibadan School of Government and Public Policy on "Getting Government to Work for Development and Democracy in Nigeria: Agenda for Change", International Conference Center, University of Ibadan, Ibadan, February 1-2, 2016.

[78] Can the Market on its own produce a resilient economy? In Osita Ogbu (2010), I stated that "Market has its efficient characteristics, but the new realities, including the inapplicability of "creative destruction", have forced the need to deepen the governance of the market. I observed that, what I called the "new market economy" would require new strong institutions, the widening of the tax base, provision for contingent liability, and robust regulatory systems (with early warning system) that are transparent, credible and effective." See Ogbu, O. (2010). "On the Global Financial Crisis, "Creative Destruction" and the "New Market Economy"", in Eboh, E. & Ogbu, O. (ed). The Global Economic Crisis and Nigeria: Taking the Right Lessons and Avoiding the Wrong Lessons._(Enugu: African Institute for Applied Economics).

[79] The discussions in this piece benefitted from Zolli, Andrew and Healy Ann Marie (2012). Resilience,_Headline Publishing Group, London

[80] In our case it would be tribes, states, regions, religious groups and other affiliations.

[81] Wilkinson, R. and Pickett, (2010). The Spirit Level: why Greater Equality Makes Societies Stronger, (New York, NY: Bloomsbury Press).

[82] Please note that this piece was written in 2012. Some of the data are outdated.

[83] This was a scheme introduced by the Buhari administration to extend small amounts of money to petty traders and other informal sector operators as palliatives.

[84] Sen, A. (2000). Development as Freedom. Anchor Books, Random House, New York.

[85] Jeffery, D.Sachs. (2006). The End of Poverty: Economic Possibilities for Our Time. (New York: Penguin Books)

[86] Ogbu, O. "Looking-In with Courage: Some Reflections on Raw Material Research and Development Council at 26, RMRDC, February, 2014.

[87] Schwartz, B & Sharpe Kenneth (2010). Practical Wisdom: The Right Way to Do the Right Thing. New York: Riverhead Books.

[88] Sen, Amartya (2007). Identity and Violence: The Illusion of Destiny. New York: W.W. Norton & Company.

[89] Tope Shola Akinyetun (2022) Bandits in Nigeria: Insights from Situational Action and Situational Crime Prevention Theories, ACCORD, March 15, 2022. www.accord.org.za referenced on June 20, 2021.

[90] Abiodun, T. F., Oladejo, O. A., Oludotun, A., Nwannennaya, C. (2019). Security Intelligence Cooperation and the Coordinated War on Terror Among Nigeria's

Security Agencies: Panacea to Stable National Security. Global Scientific Journals (GSJ): Volume 7, Issue 7, July, PP 541-556.

[91] Abiodun, T.F. et. Al. (2019) Op. Cit. P554.

[92] Federal Republic of Nigeria (2019). National Security Strategy.

[93] Frazier, R.M. (2014). "A Canon for Cooperation: A Review of Interagency Cooperation Literature". Journal of Public Administration and Governance, 4(1), 1-22. And Abiodun, T.F. et. al. op.cit.

[94] Ahmed, L. (2007). Inter-Agency Relationships. In S.E. Arase and I.P.O. Iwuofor (eds.), Policing Nigeria in the 21st Century. Ibadan: Spectrum Books Limited.

[95] Senor, Dan and Singer, Saul (2009). Start-UP Nation – The Story of Israeli's Economic Miracle. New York: Twelve Hatchette Book Group. p.118

[96] Senor and Singer (2009). Op. cit. pp. 120-121.

[97] Stemming Illicit Financial Flows from Nigeria: Is Political Will the Missing Link?, Expert Report for The Independent Corrupt Practices Commission, April 2021.

[98] United States Department of Homeland Security, Wikipedia, accessed, June 22, 2002.

[99] Ogbu, O. (2012). Toward Inclusive Growth in Nigeria, Policy Brief 2012-2013, Global View, Global Economy and Development, The Brookings Institution, Washington D.C.

[100] Acemoglu, Daron and Restrepo, Pascual (2019), "Automoation and New Tasks: How Technology Displaces and Reinstates Labor", Journal of Economics Perspectives, vol. 33, November 2, - Spring 2019 – pages 3 – 30
Rodrik, Dani (2018). "New Technologies, Global Value Chains and developing Economies", NBER Working Paper No. 25164, http//www.nber.org/papers/w25164

[101] Christensen, Clayton, Ojomo, Efosa and Dillon, Karen (2019). The Prosperity Paradox: How Innovation Can Lift Nations Out of Poverty. (Harper Collin Publishers: New York, USA).

[102] World Economic Forum (2017). "The Future of Jobs and Skills in Africa – Preparing the Region for the Fourth Industrial Revolution". Executive Briefing.

[103] Senor, Dan and Singer, Saul (2009). Start-UP Nation – The Story of Israeli's Economic Miracle. New York: Twelve Hatchette Book Group. p.289

[104] Senor, Dan and Singer, Saul (2009). Start-UP Nation – The Story of Israeli's Economic Miracle. New York: Twelve Hatchette Book Group. p.295

www.ingramcontent.com/pod-product-compliance
Lightning Source LLC
Chambersburg PA
CBHW050805270326
41926CB00025B/4545